MW01090051

TENNESSEE WOMEN
of Vision and Courage

EDITED BY
CHARLOTTE CRAWFORD AND RUTH JOHNSON SMILEY

Front cover photo *Evelyn Johnson* courtesy of Sue Johnson family photos
Back cover photo *Charlotte Crawford and Ruth Johnson Smiley*
by Michael Broyles Photography

CreateSpace Independent Publishing Platform
North Charleston, South Carolina

Never underestimate the power of dreams and the influence of the human spirit. We are all the same in this notion. The potential for greatness lives within each of us.

— Wilma Rudolph

CONTENTS

PREFACE

Tennessee Women of Vision and Courage is a compilation of stories depicting the strength, tenacity, and compassion of twenty-two Tennessee women. The stories are accounts of historic Tennessee women written by contemporary Tennessee women for the women and girls of our state to read, remember, and find inspiring.

Women have contributed significantly to Tennessee's rich heritage during our more than two-hundred-year history as a state. Yet, only a small number of these women are included in written history. Academic books and articles detail accounts of some of their lives; other outstanding women are known only to a few. Our goal is to recognize a few representative Tennessee women from frontier days though the twentieth century who faced hardship and challenges with vision and courage.

The narratives are short and easy to read by design. Yet, for those who want to learn more, there are endnote citations and references.

This book began its life as an article celebrating Women's History Month that profiled four leaders for the *AAUW Tennessean,* of which we were editors. Their stories were so impressive that we wanted to learn more. These led us to the decision that nothing less than a book would suffice.

We elicited broad-based support and involvement from women's organizations and higher education institutions across the state. Six organizations and two university groups became partners for the Tennessee Women Project. With an advisory council comprised of partner representatives and other key individuals (including a high school student), we had a network from which to solicit nominations of historic women, including those less well known, for inclusion in the book.

From the more than one hundred women nominated, we selected twenty-two. Each woman was carefully chosen based on her influence on life in Tennessee, the era in which she lived, and her geographic location, ethnicity, and vocation.

The women profiled include married women, widows, those who never married, and those who married and divorced. In some instances, women took over responsibilities for managing a household, operating a farm, or managing a business following the husband's death, a divorce, or the husband going into the military. Their experiences show strength and fortitude.

Several women's stories describe crucial times in our state's history — removal of the Cherokee Indians to Oklahoma on the Trail of Tears, abolition of slavery, and the struggle for racial justice. Other women played heroic roles in the fight for woman suffrage. Their efforts within the state led to ratification of the Nineteenth Amendment making Tennessee the thirty-sixth and final state needed for women to claim their right to vote.

For women who wanted a career during the eighteenth, nineteenth, and early twentieth centuries, the primary choice open to them was teaching. Even so, a female teacher was often required to give up her position when she married or when she had children. Few women became members of a college or university faculty.

Nonetheless, these stories include forerunners not only in education, but also in other fields including medicine, music, law, banking, newspaper publishing, science, politics, athletics, and aviation. Two women used writing and art to speak to social issues; several developed their oratorical skills. Other women contributed as homemakers and mothers — often in combination with a career. These women can serve as inspiring role models for today's young women in making their career choices.

For well-educated women who were financially secure, women's organizations provided a means for them to be involved in educational pursuits, philanthropy, and the betterment of society. These organizations enabled women to be at the forefront of social causes including woman suffrage, the temperance movement, compulsory education requirements, alleviation of poverty, civil rights, and equal opportunities for women. With more social and civic involvement, women began to think about public service and running for elected office.

These women's stories reflect historical trends and give us a perspective about significant social changes over time. We see past progress and, at the same time, realize that challenges remain.

Charlotte Crawford
Ruth Johnson Smiley

ELIZABETH PAXTON HOUSTON

1757–1831

A Pioneering Woman of Faith

DEBORAH GRACE STALEY

Courtesy of Doug Smiley

Sam Houston American Giant Homesite. In 1807, Sam Houston arrived at this 419-acre site with his widowed mother and eight brothers and sisters. —Historical Marker

Upon moving into a farmhouse that is nearly 150 years old, I began searching for information about early settlers to the Trigonia Community of Blount County where I now live. My search led me to Baker's Creek Presbyterian Church where, unexpectedly, I found the grave of Elizabeth Paxton Houston. Further exploration revealed two striking facts about this East Tennessee pioneer. First, she was the mother of the famed Sam Houston. Second, at the age of fifty, this widow left her family and the only home she'd ever known to move from Virginia to East Tennessee with her nine children. Why would this woman do such a thing?

— *DEBORAH GRACE STALEY*

Raised the daughter of Captain John and Mary Blair Paxton, the richest family in Rockbridge County, Virginia, Elizabeth could have lived the life of a genteel Southern lady. Instead, her life as a young girl centered around work on her family farm and the church.[1] The Paxtons and others in a community that included a family named Houston, settled in the area via Ulster, Ireland, and Philadelphia. These devout Presbyterians had come to America seeking freedom to practice their religion, which focused on rigid adherence to the Bible.[2] Her family valued church, hard work, and education. These were people who spent all day at church on Sundays — a practice Elizabeth would continue throughout her life.[3] Elizabeth also possessed "a highly cultivated intellect," though it is not certain if she attended school or was educated at home.[4]

In 1781, at the age of twenty-four, Elizabeth married her neighbor, a man of similar beliefs and background. The dashing Major Samuel Houston was a veteran of the Revolutionary War who served as an officer and paymaster in the celebrated Morgan's Rifle Brigade. Having no fondness for farming, the Major continued to serve as an officer after the war with the Virginia Militia, inspecting fortifications along the frontier. Never wealthy, he did inherit his family's property, Timber Ridge Plantation, which featured a two-story home with white columns and considerable land. Here Elizabeth and her husband made their home. Not so distant neighbors included George Washington, Thomas Jefferson, and James Monroe.[5]

Elizabeth had six boys and then three daughters. Sensible and strong-willed, with the help of her children, Elizabeth ran the family plantation during her husband's long absences. To her credit, the home was completely self-sufficient. Tobacco, corn, and wheat crops supplied food, with all excess sold to provide income. Elizabeth made clothing for her children from spun cloth and shoes were cobbled on site. Still, Major Houston's career strained the family finances because officers in the militia were expected to pay their own expenses.[6]

Facing financial ruin, in 1806 Major Houston visited a cousin, James Houston, in East Tennessee. The Houston fort, located on Nine Mile Creek in the present-day Calderwood Community of Blount County, had seen numerous attacks from Cherokee Indians. However, with the presence of the militia, settlers had been at peace with the Indians for more than a decade.[7] Still, this wild, unsettled land offered rich farmland that came cheap because of its proximity to the Cherokee Indian boundary. After arranging to purchase property on a branch of Baker's Creek that Major Houston referred to as "God's Country," he returned home and prepared to move his family.[8]

In order to pay off debts and purchase equipment needed for the relocation, Elizabeth's husband began selling all she had worked hard to maintain. But before the move could be made, Major Houston died unexpectedly in 1806 while on an inspection tour. Having no other choice, Elizabeth sold Timber Ridge Plantation to a neighbor for £1,000. In the spring of 1807, at the age of fifty, she packed two covered wagons with only basic necessities and left Virginia to travel the Great Warrior and Trading Path to Tennessee with her nine children who ranged in age from seven to early twenties.[9]

Elizabeth rode in the lead wagon driven by her son, Sam, with her three daughters in the back. Another son drove a second wagon that carried two female slaves and their children, while the rest of Elizabeth's sons served as armed outriders. The Houstons journeyed three weeks, averaging an impressive fifteen miles per day, over rough, treacherous terrain. Their destination would be 419 acres, with natural springs, ten miles south of Maryville. James Houston provided Elizabeth and her family with temporary aid and shelter.[10]

The family immediately began clearing property to make adequate shelter and put in crops for sustenance before winter. They built a one-story log structure on a rise overlooking the meadows of Baker's Creek. Close neighbors included the Sam Henry family, who had built a fort as well as a mill that ground corn for the community. The Henrys had also donated property in 1796 for the establishment of Baker's Creek Presbyterian Church, which would be at the center of the Houstons' new life on the frontier.[11] Built in the shape of a cross, the pulpit stood opposite an area used to store weapons while congregants worshiped. The pro-slavery congregation was integrated, welcoming both slaves and freed slaves. This frontier church addressed problems including swearing, dancing, and making and overindulging in spirits.[12]

Elizabeth Houston's life in Tennessee proved to be far from idyllic. Soon after the relocation, her oldest son, Paxton, died of consumption, and her daughter, Isabella, who was described as "sickly" also died. Elizabeth's son, Sam, vexed his mother.[13] Sam, like his father, hated farming and, unwilling to meet family expectations, ran away.[14]

Distressed, Elizabeth sent her sons to look for Sam, taking needed workers from the family farm for weeks. They found Sam ninety miles away, living on Hiwassee Island with the Cherokee.[15] On behalf of their mother, the brothers entreated Sam to come home, but Houston, in his autobiography, said that the wild liberty of the red man suited his nature far better than the restraints of the white settlements.[16] Sam stayed with the Cherokee until he was eighteen, causing the Houston family shame in the community. Sam did visit his mother when he needed clothing, which she made for him. During these visits, Sam dishonored his family further by going into Maryville, where he was known for his boisterous behavior and running up considerable debt with merchants.[17]

To pay off this debt, Elizabeth sent her son to two acquaintances who had opened a school fifteen miles from town. Andrew Kennedy and Henry McCulloch needed a headmaster and hired Sam. It speaks to Elizabeth Houston's dedication for educating her children that Sam, who had very little formal education, ably served in this capacity. During the six months Sam taught, the school flourished with record enrollment of young students and adult men. In a brief time, Sam made enough money to pay off his debts.[18]

Houston's tenure as schoolteacher ended when he volunteered as a private in the army for the War of 1812. Upon his departure, Elizabeth gave her son a musket and a gold ring engraved with the word, "honor," which he wore until his death. She was known to say to Sam, "I had rather all my sons fill one honorable grave, than that one of them should turn his back to save his life. Go, and remember, too, that while the door of my cottage is open to brave men, it is eternally shut against cowards."[19] Elizabeth Houston's fifth son became a celebrated military leader, governor and two-term congressman from Tennessee, and president and senator from Texas.[20]

Elizabeth enjoyed many visits from her famous son. However, her children had to have been a source of heartache as well as pride. Sam returned to Elizabeth's home after the Battle of Horseshoe Bend, seriously injured, having been left for dead by army physicians.[21] Brought to Elizabeth on a horse-drawn stretcher,[22] he was in such poor condition she was said to have recognized only his eyes. Undeterred, over the course of several months, Elizabeth nursed Sam back to health.[23]

Elizabeth's son, Robert, also fought in the War of 1812. However, soon after the war, he took his own life in Virginia as a result of "disappointment in a love affair." Her daughter, Mary, died in an insane asylum. Elizabeth's other children enjoyed successful lives, but all moved away from Baker's Creek, proving the family's wanderlust. James, a merchant, relocated to Nashville. John, who had been a major in the army, moved to Memphis. William became a lawyer and died in Washington City. Eliza married, but spent her final days in Texas with her brother Sam.[24]

At seventy-four, Elizabeth Paxton Houston died with her son Sam at her side. Today, the home she built on Baker's Creek no longer stands. Only two items belonging to her are on display at the Sam Houston Museum in Huntsville, Texas: her eyeglasses and a book of poetry by Robert Burns written in Scottish dialect.[25] And yet, her impact on the East Tennessee community she called home is still felt. The local chapter of the Society Children of the American Revolution is named for her. On November 8, 1942, 111 years after her death, they erected an impressive monument at Baker's Creek Presbyterian Church Cemetery to mark her resting place in a ceremony attended by the community and Houston descendants. In remarks on this occasion, the words of Judge Samuel O. Houston best sum up this exceptional woman's life. "She was gifted with intellectual and moral qualities which elevated her . . . above most of her sex. Her life shone with purity and benevolence and yet she was nerved with a stern fortitude, which never gave way."[26]

NOTES

[1] Marshall DeBruhl, *Sword of Jacinto, A Life of Sam Houston* (New York: Random House, 1993), 15.

[2] Judge Samuel O. Houston, *History of the Robert Houston Family, 1802–1865*, 1-6.

[3] DeBruhl, 12-16.

[4] General Sam Houston, *Life of General Sam Houston, A Short Autobiography* (Austin, Texas: The Pemberton Press, 1964), 1.

[5] DeBruhl, 15-20.

[6] Ibid.

[7] Alberta and Carson Brewer, *Valley So Wild, A Folk History* (Knoxville: East Tennessee Historical Society, 1975), 73-75.

[8] "The Houstons," Remarks of Mrs. Sam Houston Pickens at the Dedication of Marker in Memory of Elizabeth Paxton Houston (1942).

[9] DeBruhl, 21-24.

[10] Ibid.

[11] Ibid.

[12] "History of Baker's Creek Presbyterian Church," http://www.bakerscreekpc.org/AboutUs.aspx.

[13] Rev. Samuel Rutherford Houston, *Brief Biographical Account of Members of the Houston Family* (Cincinnati: Elm Street Printing Company, 1882), 24-35.

[14] DeBruhl, 27-31.

[15] Ibid.

[16] Mrs. John L. Brewer, Speech Given at the Dedication of the Elizabeth Paxton Houston Marker (1942), 4.

[17] General Sam Houston, 1.

[18] DeBruhl, 26-35.

[19] DeBruhl, 37-38.

[20] Judge Samuel O. Houston, 26–29.

[21] DeBruhl, 43–44.

[22] Mrs. John L. Brewer, 4.

[23] DeBruhl, 43–44.

[24] Rev. Samuel Rutherford Houston, 24–35.

[25] Lauren Schaubhut, Curator of Collections, Sam Houston Memorial Museum, interview by Deborah Grace Staley, (June 22, 2012).

[26] Judge Samuel O. Houston, *Historical Sketch of Elizabeth Paxton Houston* (1942), 6.

Elizabeth "Quatie" Brown Henley Ross

ca. 1791–1839

Her Legend of Compassion

Judy Arnold

Courtesy of the Tennessee State Library and Archives

Chattanooga Area Home of John Ross

Elizabeth Brown Henley Ross, known as Quatie,[1] is a mysterious figure in Tennessee history. She was the wife of Cherokee Principal Chief John Ross, son of the founder of Ross's Landing (now Chattanooga). Some say she was a full-blooded Cherokee from the Bird Clan. Others say she was the daughter of Thomas Brown, a mixed-blood ferry owner, or that she was the daughter of a Scottish trader and sister of Judge James Brown of the Cherokee. Whether full-blood or mixed-blood, she had a stronger Cherokee lineage than her husband who was one-eighth Cherokee,[2] and her marriage to John Ross strengthened his popularity and position with the Cherokee tribe.

Ross was principal chief from 1828 to 1866, one of the darkest periods of American history—The Trail of Tears. In the years between 1813 and 1855, the United States government forced the removal of all Native Americans living east of the Mississippi River. The forcible removal of the Cherokee from their Eastern Appalachian mountain homes to the Western Reservations was called Nunna-a-ul-tsun-yi, "The Place Where They Cried."[3]

Quatie's first husband died in the War of 1812, so Quatie was a widow with one child when she married John Ross in 1813. Quatie bore John Ross six children, one of whom died at birth.

As a political wife, Quatie cared for the children at home while John Ross went to Washington and desperately fought to keep the Cherokee on their own land. The Cherokee as well as the whites respected him—including Jacksa Chula Harjo (Andrew Jackson) with whom he had fought in the War of 1812. Because they had fought with Jackson, the Native Americans expected his support.[4] Instead, Jackson created and enforced the plan for Indian removal.

While Ross was in Washington, the situation in Georgia became desperate for the Cherokee and for Quatie who was trying to maintain their family and property alone. When Ross returned after failing to stop the plans for removal, he discovered Quatie in tears. Armed Georgia squatters had locked her and two of their children in a bedroom in their own home.[5] Squatters took the land by holding lotteries sanctioned by the Georgia governor and legislature and forced the Cherokee, including Chief Ross's family, out of Northern Georgia.[6] It was at this time that the family fled to Tennessee near Flint Springs and lived there before "The Removal."[7]

Quatie led a life of hardship. She was pregnant seven times, lost a child in childbirth, and raised six children virtually alone. She was forcibly removed from her home more than once. In bad health and travelling under horrific conditions, Quatie died on the Trail of Tears. A white traveler from Maine who passed a camp of Cherokees described the conditions on the Trail of Tears:

> Aged females, apparently nearly ready to drop into the grave, were traveling with heavy burdens attached to the back—on the frozen ground . . . with no covering for the feet except what Nature had given them. We learned from the inhabitants on the road where the Indians passed that they buried fourteen or fifteen at every stopping place. . . .[8]

Legend has it that Quatie died of exposure on the Trail of Tears after giving her blanket to a sick child. The legend comes from the moving story of her death related by John Burnett:

> The trail of the exiles was a trail of death. They had to sleep in the wagons and on the ground without fire. And I have known as many as twenty-two of them to die in one night of pneumonia due to ill treatment, cold, and exposure. Among this number was the beautiful Christian wife of Chief John Ross. This noble-hearted woman died a martyr to childhood,

giving her only blanket for the protection of a sick child. She rode thinly clad through a blinding sleet and snowstorm, developed pneumonia, and died in the still hours of a bleak winter night, with her head resting on Lieutenant Gregg's saddle blanket. . . . Her uncoffined body was buried in a shallow grave by the roadside far from her native mountain home, and the sorrowing cavalcade moved on.[9]

While the spirit of Private Burnett's account is accurate, Quatie's family has discounted the tale because it was an embellished story told on Burnett's eighty-fifth birthday long after the actual event. Moreover, he made claims about his own status and facts of the trip that were not true. One contradiction was his account that Quatie was buried in an unmarked grave by the side of the road. Her burial place remains a mystery because there are varying accounts, all of which claim to be factual. There is another unsubstantiated claim that Quatie is buried in Little Rock, Arkansas, in one of the town's early cemeteries and that a picture of her grave marker can be seen on the web.[10]

Quatie's great-great-grandson, Bruce Ross, commented on the blanket legend and the dispute about her burial:

In *The Arkansas Gazette* of February 2, 1839, it reports her passing on the Arkansas River near Little Rock. There's speculation that she is buried in the Mt. Holly Cemetery in downtown Little Rock. I do NOT believe this to be true. There is a memorial stone there, but it is in the Albert Pike lot next to Pike's wife. I hardly believe that any member of my family would allow her to be interred anywhere near Pike or his family. Pike and Ross were diametrically opposed to the other's politics. As for the blanket story — that's just what I believe it is, a story.[11]

The great-great-great granddaughter of Quatie, Gayle Ross, stated that Quatie was ill for two years preceding the Trail of Tears and that she died on a boat.[12] Other sources confirm that Quatie was on the ship, *Victoria*, with her husband and some 228 other people when she died.[13] John Ehle marries the two stories, claiming that even on the river route there was a passage of land to cross.[14] Whatever the details of her death, Quatie died in what John Burnett called the "most brutal order in the history of American warfare."

Bruce Ross writes his explanation of why so little is known about his great-great-grandmother:

> I have read the Papers of Chief John Ross (a compilation of all known communiques both to and from him throughout his life) and there are countless letters to and from him and his second wife, Mary Brian Stapler. I have been asked many times as to why there are none between him and Quatie. The only possible conclusion I could arrive at, is that she couldn't read nor write, so why would there be? She bore him six children, and I believe she was dedicated to Motherhood, and to family life with no interest outside the home.[15]

Quatie's legacy lives in her personal story as wife and mother and as a victim of the Trail of Tears. Subsequent generations of strong women emerged from her family. Gayle Ross is a noted storyteller. Mary Golda Ross was the first woman and first Native American aeronautical engineer to work with the American space program, contributing to defense and space exploration efforts.[16] Jennie Ross

Cobb, a photographer and the first Director/Curator of the Murrell Home, was another well-known member of the family.[17]

Quatie Ross left a proud Cherokee heritage important to Tennessee history. In 2005, at a ceremony in Chattanooga opening "The Passage," a pedestrian walkway between downtown and the Tennessee River, Principal Chief Chad Smith said, "We are not a people of the past. We are a people of the present and for many centuries; we will be a people of the future."[18] The legacy of accomplishments of Quatie Ross's descendants, as well as her own example of Cherokee courage, gives support to this proud statement.

NOTES

[1] According to descendant Bruce Ross, her name was pronounced "Quay-te." The name Quatie is Cherokee for Betty or Betsy.

[2] Gary E. Moulton, *John Ross: Cherokee Chief* (Athens: University of Georgia Press, 1978), 12-13.

[3] Theda Perdue and Michael D. Green, *The Cherokee Nation and The Trail of Tears* (New York: Viking, 2007), 68.

[4] Ibid., 59-61.

[5] Gloria Jahoda, *The Trail of Tears: The Story of the American Indian Removals, 1813-1855* (New York: Random House, 1973), 219.

[6] Ibid., 219-220.

[7] Bruce Ross, e-mail message to Judy Arnold, June 19, 2012.

[8] Jahoda, 273.

[9] *"Guthrie Studios: The Trail of Tears: The Birthday Story of Private John G. Burnett. 1838-1839,"* accessed May 29, 2012. http://www.guthriestudios.com/Private%20John%20Burnett.htm.

[10] "John Burnett's Account," *The Chronicles of Oklahoma* 80, 3 (2002): 337-341.

[11] Bruce Ross, e-mail message to Judy Arnold, June 4, 2012.

[12] "'Cherokee Moses' comes home," modified January 2010, http://clairesawers.com/.

13 "Archive Record," modified December 29, 2011. http:// cherokeemuseum.pastperfect-online.com/3536cgi/mweb. exe?request=record;id=241#5834-7C92-41F9-A7BB-132523914381;type=3011.

14 Ibid.

15 Bruce Ross, e-mail message to Judy Arnold, June 4, 2012.

16 "Miscellaneous Ramblings," modified May 20, 2012. http://www. kuwiskuwi.net/Misc..html.

17 Bruce Ross, e-mail message to Judy Arnold, June 19, 2012. Bruce Ross, himself a former Chief of the Seven Clan Council, reports the successes of the men and women in his generation. "We've had a postmaster, six teachers (science, music, librarian, elementary, secondary), three farmers, one retired commercial airline pilot, one aerospace engineer, one state traffic engineer, three federal employees, a BIA loan officer, three housewives (hardest job of all)."

18 Perdue and Green, 163-164.

Frances "Fanny" Wright

1795–1852

Wedded to Human Improvement

Sara Baker

1881, John Chester Buttre, Engraver
Prints and Photographs division, Library of Congress, Washington, DC

Frances "Fanny" Wright

F rances Wright was neither born nor raised in Tennessee, but her work in the state was certainly significant. Six feet tall, with curly auburn hair, a rich voice, and a dynamic personality, she was bound to stand out among the delicate women of her time. Wright became a pioneer in equal rights who created a planned community in Tennessee where residents with shared beliefs on racial equality worked toward the goal of emancipation. Although her intentional community, Nashoba, ultimately failed, it served as a model for anti-slavery utopias for years to come.[1]

Wright's travels throughout America in 1824 convinced her that slavery was abominable and "emancipation without expatriation . . . seem[ed] impossible."[2] She visited New Harmony, Indiana, an intentional community developed by Robert Owen, who had established similar experiments in Wright's hometown of Glasgow, Scotland, and held membership in the Glasgow Literary Society with Wright's uncle, moral philosopher James Mylne. She began to see an alternative to the slave system embedded in American culture and economics. Emboldened by New Harmony, she set out to start her own commune wherein she would train slaves to become self-sufficient as they worked off their debt, preventing the economic collapse that most saw as an inevitable part of ending free labor. With the support of Thomas Jefferson and influential Tennesseans such as Andrew Jackson and Memphis's first mayor, Marcus B. Winchester, she acquired thirty slaves and two thousand acres outside of Memphis, calling the experiment Nashoba, the Chickasaw word for "wolf," because it lay alongside the Wolf River. In addition to Jackson's interest in gradual emancipation, Wright may have chosen Tennessee because it was the home of Elihu Embree's *The Emancipator*, the first paper devoted exclusively to the abolition of slavery, and several anti-slavery groups.

Wright envisioned a self-supporting community that would raise money to purchase and train additional slaves. She drew on the principles behind New Harmony—liberty, equality, and community—and expanded them by ensuring that black children would attend school with whites and emphasizing women's rights. She wrote, "No woman can forfeit her individual rights or independent existence, and no man assert over her any power whatsoever."[3] In theory at least, Nashoba was more dedicated to women's rights than any other nineteenth-century commune.[4]

Wright was unable to fully implement her grand ideas, however, as the community disbanded by 1828. English novelist Frances Trollope wrote about Nashoba's poorly built structures and lack of food and water, describing how Wright "stood in the midst of all this desolation, with the air of a conqueror."[5] A combination of bad luck and ill preparation doomed the project: mosquito-infested swampland, crop failure, lack of experience, disease, ineffective leadership while Wright was away, and little support for true integration. In response to public outcry over interracial relationships in Nashoba, Wright wrote an article advocating integration, which only stoked the uproar, concerning both Nashoba's supporters and neighbors. Although she had invested more than half of her fortune and her own hard labor, she finally gave up and helped the workers secure new lives in Haiti in 1830, even traveling with them to Port-au-Prince. Despite its lack of true equality and eventual demise, Nashoba inspired similar communities, which were responsible for freeing three to five thousand slaves prior to the Civil War.

A combination of education, a decent inheritance, highly developed principles, and impressive fortitude led this stately, outspoken Scotswoman to make her mark in Tennessee and American history. Known as Fanny, Wright was orphaned not long after her birth on February 6, 1795, in Dundee, Scotland. Aristocratic relatives in

England raised her and her sister, Camilla, until 1816, when they returned to Scotland to live with their uncle, the moral philosopher James Mylne. Disillusioned with British politics and given access to the University of Glasgow Library and Mylne's network of thinkers, Wright read voraciously about American politics, and works by Thomas Jefferson and his compatriots greatly influenced the direction of her life. She later said in her famous Independence Day speech at New Harmony Hall in 1828, "The frame of federative government that sprung out of the articles signed in '76, is one of the most beautiful inventions of the human intellect."[6]

At age twenty-three, with only Camilla by her side, Wright traveled to America for the first time, starting in New York. There she became the first woman to have a play, *Altorf*, produced on the American stage. In 1821, she published *Views of Society and Manners in America*, noting that women in America were "assuming their place as thinking beings."[7] The book became one of the most popular travel memoirs of the period. In fact, Wright was such an effective writer that she struck up a friendship through letters with Thomas Jefferson, who admired her talent and values. When she published *A Few Days in Athens*, a fictional tale based on the work of Epicurus, Jefferson declared it "equal to the best morsels of antiquity."[8]

As an independent and fiercely intelligent woman, Wright drew a number of admirers, including writer Mary Shelley, economist John Stuart Mill, reformer Jeremy Bentham, and the Marquis de Lafayette. She and Lafayette became fast friends and developed a father-daughter relationship, inspiring and learning from each other, although his family worried about their intimacy. Lafayette invited the Wright sisters on his farewell tour of America in 1824, meeting them at Monticello after writing to Jefferson:

[Y]ou and I are the two men in the world the esteem of whom she values the most. I wish much, my dear friend, to present these two adopted daughters of mine to Mrs. Randolph and to you; they being orphans from their youth, and preferring American principles to British aristocracy, having an independent, tho not very large fortune, have passed the three last years in most intimate connection with my children and myself.[9]

Thus, Wright finally met the author of the document that drew her to America in the first place, later saying that she "treasured" her time at Monticello as "among the most interesting of [her life]."[10]

Not everyone at Monticello shared Jefferson's enchantment with this peculiar woman, however. Jefferson relative Jane Blair Cary described her as "masculine, measuring at least 5 feet 11 inches . . . her large blue eyes and blonde aspect were thoroughly English, and she always seems to wear the wrong attire."[11] Cary reported that Wright refused to speak to women other than her hostess, Martha Jefferson Randolph, and "the Frenchmen told many instances of her masculine proclivities," which included scolding men in public for their behavior. At the time, an accusation of "masculinity" would be the last thing most women would want, especially in the South, but Wright fought for equal footing with men.

While Nashoba may have been Wright's big experiment in Tennessee, it was hardly her only egalitarian pursuit in America. She became the first woman journal editor when she joined the *Harmony Gazette,* later renamed *The Free Enquirer,* and the first woman to present a lecture series to an audience of both men and women, beginning with her 1828 Independence Day speech. Wright supported the Working Men's Party, the first labor political party in the country, which opponents dubbed "the Fanny Wright party." She actively promoted equal rights, equal education, and free love and criticized capital punishment, organized religion, and marriage. A champion for equality, Wright always believed herself to be a peer of men; once writing to Lafayette, "[T]he mind has no sex but what habit and education give it."[12] Because of her audacity to step outside of the confines of traditional femininity, opponents attacked her as the "Red Harlot of Infidelity." Jefferson's daughter Ellen Coolidge called her "this unsexed thing," saying, "I feel mortified, as a woman, as having formerly been a personal acquaintance."[13]

Since Wright's reputation threatened the Working Men's Party in the 1830 elections, she returned to Europe with Camilla, who died soon after. Distraught, Wright sought solace in the arms of Guillame Sylvan Casimir Phiquepal d'Arusmont, a French physician whom she married at age thirty-six, rather late for that period, after becoming pregnant with a daughter, Sylva. She lived a private life with her family for a brief time, but her commitment to American democracy pushed her back into the public sphere. In 1835, family in tow, she once again made the long journey to America. The d'Arusmonts found a home in Cincinnati, and Wright's lectures continued. In 1848, she published *England, the Civilizer*, her final book, in which she blamed the faults of governments on so-called masculine aggression. Where she once saw a beacon of hope, she now admitted a "complicated system of errors" regarding humanity in general.[14] Two years later, she and d'Arusmont divorced. Her views on America had dimmed, and perhaps her many disappointments — Nashoba, her sister's death, an unfulfilled marriage — wilted her optimism.

Wright died in 1852 and was buried in Cincinnati's historic Spring Grove Cemetery, where her tombstone reads, in her own words: "I have wedded the cause of human improvement, staked my fortune on it, my reputation and my life." Indeed, Walt Whitman wrote of her, "She was a brilliant woman, of beauty and estate, who was never satisfied unless she was busy doing good — public good, private good." Wright's tireless work sparked the initial stirrings of three long but fruitful movements: labor, women's, and civil rights. She was an innovator and an agitator, setting in motion long-term cultural change at great personal cost. The land where she ran her great experiment is located near present-day Germantown, Tennessee, a suburb of Memphis, and businesses, organizations, and a major thoroughfare in the area today bear the name Nashoba.

NOTES

[1] Also called communes, intentional communities, where people with a common cause come together to live out their social, religious, or political vision, became popular in the nineteenth century.

[2] Frances Wright to Julia and Harriet Garnett, November 12, 1824, Garnett Letters, Houghton Library, Harvard University.

[3] Frances Wright, "Nashoba," *New Harmony Gazette,* vol. III, no. 17 (New Harmony, Indiana: February 6, 1828).

[4] Carol A. Kolmerton, *Women in Utopia: The Ideology of Gender in the American Owenite Communities* (Bloomington: Indiana University Press, 1990).

[5] Frances Milton Trollope, *Domestic Manners of the Americans* (London: Whittaker, Treacher & Co, 1832), 29.

[6] Frances Wright, "Address I," *Course of Popular Lectures as Delivered by Frances Wright* (New York: Free Enquirer, 1829), 171-182.

[7] Frances Wright, *Views of Society and Manners in America* (London: Longman, Hurst, Rees, Long, and Brown, 1821), 218.

[8] Thomas Jefferson to Marquis de Lafayette, November 4, 1823, in *Memoir, Correspondence, and Miscellanies from the Papers of Thomas Jefferson,* vol. 4, 2nd ed., ed. Thomas Jefferson Randolph (Boston: Gray and Bowen, 1830), 383-386.

[9] Marquis de Lafayette to Thomas Jefferson, October 1, 1824, in *The Letters of Lafayette and Jefferson,* ed. Gilbert Chinard (Baltimore: Johns Hopkins Press, 1929), 421.

[10] Frances Wright to Martha Jefferson Randolph, December 4, 1824, Jefferson Papers, Library of Congress.

[11] Jane Blair Cary Smith, "Carysbrook Memoir 1880-1885," The Carys of Virginia, Accession #1378, Special Collections, University of Virginia Library, University of Virginia, Charlottesville, Virginia, 72-74.

[12] Frances Wright to Marquis de Lafayette, February 11, 1822, quoted in Lloyd Kramer, *Lafayette in Two Worlds* (Chapel Hill: University of North Carolina Press, 1996), 158.

[13] Ellen Coolidge to Martha Randolph, June 6, 1830, Ellen Wayles Randolph Coolidge Correspondence, University of Virginia.

[14] Frances Wright, *Address on the State of the Public Mind and the Measures Which it Calls For* (New York: Free Enquirer, 1829), 7-8.

Angie Villette Warren Perkins

1854–1921

Education Advocate for All

Kathy Owens Duggan

Courtesy of Duggan Family

Angie Villette Warren Perkins

A t a time when few women received formal schooling, Angie Warren Perkins worked hard to make education accessible not only to women, but to all people. Forming clubs dedicated to furthering learning, women like Angie organized to write letters and articles to convince legislators that everyone deserved an education, regardless of race, sex, or economic status. These women's arguments helped convince men of the need for social reforms.

Angie worked tirelessly and without pay. She led by example, renouncing the militant approach to social justice that was popular. Her work ethic, oral skills, and encouraging demeanor endeared her to the community, and earned her the respect of prominent men who had the power to make social changes.[1] Many notable women go unnoticed because they do not seek self-recognition. Angie Warren Perkins was such a woman. Her accomplishments included educator, politician, writer, and volunteer, while serving as a devoted wife and mother of four. However, her passion was education. During her sixty-seven years, she advocated for making affordable education accessible to all.

Born November 6, 1854, in Killingly, Connecticut, to Lysander and Marcia Mason Warren, Angie enjoyed life in an education-oriented family. Her father was regarded as one of the most "public-spirited and progressive men" of his time. In spite of not completing his college education, he became a public servant who dedicated thirty years to the board of education and three terms as a Connecticut state legislator.[2] Angie followed his example.

Education advocates had touted compulsory education in New England since 1650, but schools were still scarce during Angie's early years. At age fourteen Angie attended a boarding school, where she was an apt scholar. She witnessed firsthand the everyday struggle for a better life while walking past children on their way to factory jobs.[3] This was the industrial age when children worked in factories or on farms rather than attending school. By 1872, the Connecticut compulsory education law sent children to school instead of into the labor force.

Angie was the first of four women to graduate from Wesleyan University in Middleton, Connecticut, in 1876.[4] She taught briefly at a high school before returning to Wesleyan for a master's degree. She served as a professor of French and Latin at Wellesley College and later became preceptress[5] and teacher of French and history at Lawrence University in Wisconsin.

At Lawrence, Angie fell in love with Charles Perkins, professor of mathematics, and the two married and had three children. In 1892, Charles assumed the position of associate professor of physics and electricity at the University of Tennessee. Their fourth child, Warren, was born in Knoxville in 1894.

After her marriage, Angie put aside her own career to advance that of her husband. As a professor's wife, she used her social skills to further women's causes through university circles.

Angie befriended Lizzie Crozier French, an educator and driving force in the woman suffrage movement. French founded Ossoli Circle, the oldest women's club in Tennessee, and Angie became president of Ossoli in 1896. Clubs for women were strong in Knoxville, and under Angie's leadership, Ossoli organized the Tennessee Federation of Women's Clubs. The goal was for clubwomen to unite to build philosophical arguments to convince legislators to provide educational opportunities for everyone. While French traveled the country making speeches for women's rights, Angie took a subtler path. She felt that men were unconvinced of women's competencies outside the home. She used her wit, intellect, and powers of persuasion to convince men of women's capabilities.[6]

Angie's charismatic, hardworking, and progressive nature earned her a strong reputation in the community. The University of Tennessee student newspaper, *Orange and White,* noted, "She was a friend to all under all circumstances," and "never allowed anyone to feel her superiority."[7] Dr. Charles Dabney, president of the University and an advocate of higher education for women, was impressed with Angie's education, determination, and charm, and eagerly sought her advice in matters involving coeducation.[8] In 1893, one year after their alliance, women were admitted to the University of Tennessee.[9]

In 1897, Angie accepted the position of dean of women without pay. She helped form the women's department at the University of Tennessee, and served until a paid dean was appointed in 1900. She then resumed her club work full time.[10]

Angie and her husband enhanced the family education with extensive travel. They toured widely throughout the United States, and explored foreign countries. While traveling they interacted with the local people. To share these experiences, Angie wrote journal articles accompanied by her own illustrations. The articles, published in local newspapers, were compiled into two books: *From San Diego to Sitka* and *Our Year Abroad.*[11]

In 1896, Tennessee was almost "the last of illiterate states" because of a large number of uneducated people, many of whom lived in the Smoky and Cumberland Mountains.[12] Angie began mountain settlement work. Through the Tennessee Federation of Women's Clubs, she organized traveling libraries, schoolhouses, and social services. She wrote, "The torch of education was held high over the valleys, lighting up the gloom of ignorance, the darkness of superstition, sending hope into hopeless hearts and planting seeds of ambition that rapidly bore fruit."[13] To raise money, she tirelessly made speeches, wrote articles, and contributed from personal funds.[14]

Angie's leadership as president of the General Federation of Women's Clubs from 1904–1906 was instrumental in presenting the compulsory education bill to the Tennessee legislature. She worked extremely hard on this bill because of her experiences with the mountain people. Her family loved the mountains, but the poverty touched her deeply. In 1905, the bill passed. A compulsory attendance bill followed, which passed in 1913.[15] Education was now available, and parents were accountable for their children's attendance. This was a huge step for Tennesseans.

In a 1901 dedication speech for Barbara Blount Hall, the first women's hall at the University of Tennessee, Angie said that women were learning "not to mix feelings with opinions, and not to be hurt when voted down solidly; and they have learned that the hearthstone is no less sacred because intelligence reigns there."[16]

No women could serve on school boards in Tennessee, so Angie lobbied the legislature to approve their appointment. In 1915, voters elected her to the Knoxville School Board, making her the first woman board member south of the Ohio River. For the first time in Tennessee, women had an equal voice in educational policy.

Angie united women through her network of friends in women's organizations. In addition to club work, she was director of the YWCA, regent of Daughters of the American Revolution, a founder of AAUW Knoxville and several literary societies, and a member of the Knoxville Artist's Guild. In 1921, the *Orange and White* said that she was "identified with more organizations than any woman in the city" of Knoxville.[17] Her life's passion was to instill lifelong learning in others and she made this possible by organizing women.

In January 1921, while being driven home in a snowstorm from her ninth engagement of the day, a trolley collided with their vehicle, injuring Angie. She died at home two days later. The *Orange and White* newspaper stated, "You could take 1000 women out

of Knoxville, and not all of them would equal Mrs. Perkins."
Remembered for her work ethic, high character, and her generous
spirit, Angie Warren Perkins' legacy reaches far beyond Tennessee.[18]
She was a role model and pioneer for education who understood
that great work takes a united effort.

NOTES

[1] Sadie Boyd Saxon and Elizabeth Skaggs Bowman, *Ossoli Circle Chronological History 1885–1960* (Knoxville, 1960).

[2] *Commemorative Biographical Record of Tolland and Windham Counties Connecticut* (Chicago: J. H. Beers, 1903), 524-535. Lysander walked miles through the woods to an algebra tutor to prepare himself for higher education. He struggled to attend Brown University for a few years, but family responsibilities forced him to return to the farm. Possibly due to Lysander Warren's influence, Connecticut was the sixth state to pass a compulsory education law in 1872.

[3] Angie Warren Perkins, Letter to a Cousin in Washington, DC, from Daniellsonville, Connecticut, 1868.

[4] Gerald Gaither, "Coeducation at UT," *The Tennessee Alumnus*, Fall 1974, 22-25.

[5] A preceptress was similar to a principal. The term could also mean a teacher.

[6] *Tennessee History Classroom, A Woman's Right to Vote, The Story of Lizzie Crozier French,* http://www.tennesseehistory.com/class/LizzieCrozier.htm, accessed July 6, 2012.

[7] *Orange and White*, 1921.

[8] Ibid.

[9] James Riley Montgomery, Stanley J. Folmsbee, and Lee Seifert Green, *To Foster Knowledge: A History of the University of Tennessee, 1794–1970* (Knoxville: University of Tennessee), 11-12. Five women studied at UT in the early 1800's although no degrees were awarded.

[10] It is unknown why Angie accepted the position without pay. In Gaither's "Coeducation at UT" in *The Tennessee Alumnus*, he states that she served until a permanent dean could be found.

[11] Angie Warren Perkins, *From San Diego to Sitka, 1902* was a softcover book. *Our Year Abroad, 1907* (Boston: Gorham, 1907), was hardcover.

[12] Saxon, 1960.

[13] Angie Warren Perkins, "Women's Work in Tennessee," Tennessee Federation of Women's Clubs (Memphis: Jones-Briggs Company, 1916).

[14] Saxon, 1960.

[15] Ibid.

[16] Tennessee Federation of Women's Clubs 1916. This speech also appeared in the *Knoxville Journal and Tribune,* as documented in *Ossoli Circle: Chronological History, 1885–1960.* Although a copy of the newspaper article has not been found, Angie's original draft with handwritten notes is in the family archives.

[17] *Orange and White,* 1921.

[18] Ibid.

JULIA BRITTON HOOKS

1852–1942

Sweet Notes of Influence

SHERRI GARDNER HOWELL

Berea College Photographic Archives,
Special Collections & Archives
Hutchin Library, Berea College

Julia Britton Hooks

Julia Britton Hooks had a fire burning in her heart. Her talent on the piano was incredible, garnering her press as a musical prodigy and Kentucky's wonder child. This well-educated, accomplished African American musician, born in 1852, performed publically the works of Mozart, Beethoven, Weber, and others by the age of nine. This child prodigy, however, would not be content to lead a pampered life entertaining others. She believed, taught, and lived a life that showed we all have a duty to our country and ourselves.

The daughter of free parents, Henry Britton and Laura Marshall Britton, Julia was born in Frankfort, Kentucky. Her father was a carpenter, and her mother was an accomplished singer and musician. One of her contemporaries, James T. Haley, wrote in the *Afro-American Encyclopedia*, "Her parents were free, and standing high in the social scale of their race, were greatly esteemed and respected by the aristocracy of Lexington, and she and her mother were often seen and heard in parlor concerts by the very highest society."[1] Julia Ann Amanda Morehead Britton Wertles Hooks could have enjoyed a quiet, somewhat privileged life for a young African American woman of the mid-1800s.

Julia's mother was born a slave, but was liberated by her owner at the age of sixteen. Julia and her sister, Mary Britton, were sent to Louisville, Kentucky, to the William Gibson's School of Colored Youths for one year, coming home in 1860 as unrest and war loomed on the horizon. Mary later became the first female African American physician in Kentucky. In 1869, Julia Britton enrolled in Berea College in an interracial program that not only allowed her to study music, but also to instruct white students in piano. By doing so, she became one of the first African Americans to attend college in Kentucky, and the first African American teacher at Berea College.[2] She was graduated from Berea College and moved to Greenville,

Mississippi, to teach school. She married Sam Wertles, but he died in 1873 in the yellow fever epidemic. In 1876, Julia Britton Wertles moved to Memphis, Tennessee, to teach school. There she met and married Charles Hooks.

The love of music fueled some of Julia Hooks' accomplishments. In 1883, she and Anna Church launched the Liszt-Mullard Club to raise scholarship money for promising black musicians and to promote a love of classical music. She founded the Hooks School of Music, and later, dissatisfied with the public educational opportunities for Memphis black children, she opened the Hooks Cottage School in 1892, teaching kindergarten and elementary classes.

The fire burning in Julia Hooks, however, had even deeper notes than the music she loved. Fueled at the knees of her mother, Julia Hooks sought and fought for social change for African Americans. Her mother, described as "nearly white" in color, would hold singing classes for slaves and then teach the slave children to read from "their old blue back speller hid in false pockets." As Julia and her mother traveled to present concerts, Julia would sometimes have to call her mother "Miss Laura," to keep them from trouble because of the difference in their coloring.[3]

Julia Hooks' oft-used phrase was "duty of the hour."[4] She instructed her children and grandchildren in the importance of accepting their responsibility for fighting injustices and wrongs they witnessed. Julia fought against the Jim Crow segregation of her day and racial inequality. Her grandson Benjamin Hooks, who was the executive director of the National Association for the Advancement of Colored People from 1977 to 1992, remembers that grandmother Julia was sometimes arrested for violating Jim Crow laws.[5] Once, in a Memphis theater, Julia Hooks sat in the main section of the theater and refused to move to the "colored balcony." She was physically removed by two police officers and fined five dollars.

Her interpretation of "duty of the hour" was strong on personal responsibility for self-improvement, both personally and as a collective country. Her essay "The Duty of the Hour" was published in the 1885 book *Afro-American Encyclopaedia*. In it, Julia writes of the importance of personal character building for young African Americans. She writes of the darkness of slavery, ignorance, and superstition, of the long and hard struggle, and of the thousands of miles that separate African Americans from their birthplace. But, she writes:

> America is our home. The Southland, the most beautiful part of this great Republic, is the native home of the greatest number of our race. Here floats the same banner, with its many stripes and stars, the same which has rustled above our heads for many years, differing only in the fact that its many folds are wider, its glittering stars have increased in number; and though once we could only look in anguish and sorrow upon it as it waved gently above us, we can now look upon its beautiful colors as free American citizens.[6]

To her people, Julia was a voice of encouragement and a proponent of peaceful solutions. In words that are as eloquent and thought provoking today as they were in the 1800s, Julia Hooks wrote:

> We have no great reason to be discouraged, cast down, nor hopeless about our future, because of the many unfavorable happenings; we must not expect to be entirely free from the struggles necessary to be encountered to reach true greatness.

It is our duty to use every possible and legitimate effort to avert dangers and troubles. We are earnestly persuaded to believe that the brightness of the future glory of the Negro of America is heightened by the darkness of the present clouds. . . . Character building is to be considered the "Duty of the Hour."[7]

This remarkable woman led by example. Her manner is described as dignified and compassionate, with a sincerity and gentleness that inspired trust. Her charity and influence reached into the lives of the elderly, orphans, and juvenile delinquents. She was a charter member of both the Colored Old Folks Home (later Hooks-Edwards Rest Home) and the Orphan Home Club, established in 1891. These institutions provided shelter for elderly black women and orphans. Charles Hooks was a truant officer and, in 1902, he and Julia established a juvenile court for African American offenders, locating a detention home next door to their own home and supervising it. In 1917, an escaping juvenile killed Charles Hooks, but Julia Hooks continued to provide counseling and guidance to the juvenile facility. One well-known Memphis juvenile judge, Judge Camille Kelly, would invite Julia Hooks to sit with her on certain cases that involved African American youth. Her works for the indigent and suppressed people of Memphis earned her the nickname "The Angel of Beale Street."[8]

Hooks' influence reached beyond her life in the people she worked to empower and embrace. She worked to help Blanche Kelso Bruce in his election to the US Senate where he became the first non-white senator to serve a full term. She supported Ida B. Wells, African American journalist and editor who documented lynching in the United States, and was in Memphis when Wells left to move to Chicago because of threats to her life. One of her music students was W. C. Handy, who went on to be known as the "Father of the Blues." Her family's accomplishments included a new family business, Hooks Brothers Photographers, begun by her sons Henry and Robert and continued by her grandsons, Charles and Henry, Jr. Her sons were active in promoting prominent African Americans for public office and positions, including signing a petition to endorse Robert Church, Jr., for surveyor of customs for the Port of Memphis in 1908. In addition to his role with the NAACP, grandson Benjamin Hooks was also the first African-American member of the Federal Communications Commission, appointed in 1972.

Julia Hooks died in 1942, at age ninety. The family obituary reported that she was still playing the piano a few weeks before she died.

NOTES

[1] James T. Haley, *Afro-American Encyclopaedia: Or, the Thoughts, Doings, and Sayings of the Race* (Haley & Florida, 1895), 563.

[2] Ann Mary Quarandillo, "Founders' Day Honors Angel of Beale Street," Berea College Magazine, Winter, 2002, accessed June 2, 2012, http://www.berea.edu/publications/bereacollegemagazine/archives/winter2002/winter2002(Founders'Day).asp.

[3] James T. Haley, 564.

[4] "Duty of the Hour," The Benjamin L. Hooks Institute for Social Change, accessed June 11, 2012, www.benhooks.org.

[5] Ann Mary Quarandillo, http://www.berea.edu/publications/bereacollegemagazine/archives/winter2002/winter2002(Founders'Day).asp.

[6] James T. Haley, 332.

[7] Ibid., 333.

[8] Ann Mary Quarandillo, http://www.berea.edu/publications/bereacollegemagazine/archives/winter2002/winter2002(Founders'Day).asp.

EMMA BELL MILES

1879–1919

Spirit of the Mountains

STEPHANIE TODD

Jean Miles Catino Collection, Special Collections,
University of Tennessee at Chattanooga

Emma Bell Miles

Emma Bell was born on October 19, 1879, to schoolteachers Martha Ann Mirick Bell and Benjamin Franklin Bell in Evansville, Indiana. Even in early childhood, Emma loved spending time in the woods. When frequent illness kept her from school, she would take nature walks with her mother, who taught her about the local flora and fauna. An avid reader and writer even in her youth, Emma would depict the wilderness scenes from her explorations in her sketchbook, and her love of nature, art, and literature would come to define Emma in adulthood.[1]

When Emma was ten years old, the Bells moved to what is now Red Bank, Tennessee, in search of a healthier climate for their daughter, whose poor health would continue to plague her for the rest of her life. Quickly, the family settled into the Walden's Ridge community in the Appalachian Mountains near Chattanooga. Emma soon grew to love the nature here as much as she did in Evansville, and she became quite popular with her neighbors on the mountain.

As a young woman, Emma found love on Walden's Ridge with Frank Miles. They spent hours together exploring the mountains and enjoying the wilderness of their home. This young love, however, was not well received by Emma's family and friends, who feared she would settle for life as a mountain wife, rather than pursue a career as an artist.

By the time she reached early adulthood, Emma had become well known in the Chattanooga community and much admired for her artistic talents among the locals. In 1899, with the assistance of some wealthy patrons, Emma left Walden's Ridge to attend the St. Louis School of Art. While there, Emma wrote not only of her artistic endeavors but also of her increasing love for literature, particularly her discovery of Thoreau, whose nature-themed works made Emma long for home in her beloved mountains. Adding to her longing, the distance from Frank proved difficult for Emma, and they exchanged increasingly passionate love letters. Their young romance continued to grow during the summer when she returned home from school, despite the very vocal disapproval from friends and family. So, in 1901, shortly after the death of her mother, Emma returned to Walden's Ridge and wed Frank Miles.

In spite of her strong love for Frank, Emma soon found that her life as his wife was not easy. The young couple struggled financially, at times having no place to live and little food on the table. Frank was often out of work, leaving Emma to support them with her often meager and inconsistent earnings. Additionally, her career as an artist and author exposed Emma to a more sophisticated urban life in Chattanooga, which was often at odds with her difficult home situation in the mountains. She struggled to reconcile her love of the natural world on Walden's Ridge, which was unsophisticated and hard, to her enjoyment of the comfort and refinement of the city. She writes in 1907 of "making almost superhuman efforts to get out of this intolerable situation."[2] Like her fluctuating attitude about mountain life, Emma's marital feelings toward Frank went back and forth between love and hate. At times, she was crazy about her "good man"; at others, she lamented his laziness, crude mannerisms, and inability to provide for his family.[3] However, while there were periods of separation and talks of divorce, Emma loved Frank and never renounced her decision to choose a life with him over any other.

Emma and Frank raised five children together. The first two, twin girls, came in September 1902, just before Emma's twenty-third birthday. By the time she was thirty, Emma had given birth to three more children. While childbirth was difficult for Emma and providing for a family of seven increased their financial burden, Emma found great joy in her children. In a letter to a friend in 1918, just a year before her death, she recollects, "Do you know what is

41

my greatest delight in these lonely days and nights of inaction? . . . They are just the dear, funny, foolish little unexpected remarks that my children made when they were little."[4] As much as she loved her children, giving birth to them and working to put food on the table took a physical toll on Emma.

While demanding, that same hard mountain life also provided her greatest artistic inspiration. Emma loved the Walden's Ridge wilderness more than any other space, and her life's work was dedicated to depicting, protecting, and sharing its beauty. In order to earn a living, Emma would sketch mountain scenes on postcards and begrudgingly sell them to tourists. While Emma loved her mountains and their beauty, she resented the increased tourism she saw there, fearing the development would destroy the nature and culture of the area. It was this concern that spurred Emma to become more outspoken, through writings and lectures, against the development of Walden's Ridge and the destruction of its wilderness.

Since childhood, Emma had been an avid and versatile writer. A diarist, poet, journalist, and author, Emma led a prolific life. Her short stories and poems often focused on rural life and offered readers a realistic peek into the daily lives of true mountaineers. Her works were printed in such notable publications as *Harper's Monthly* and *Putnam's Magazine* and, like her art, helped support her family. Emma's fiction was not just for entertainment, however. She believed that the unique quality of life on Walden's Ridge and in the Appalachian Mountains was at risk because of increased tourism and development. Her writing both detailed the rustic beauty of a life shared with nature and asserted that the invasion of city life was devastating, not valuable, to Appalachia.

In 1905, Emma published her most well-known work, *The Spirit of the Mountains*, a celebration of the uniqueness of Appalachian life and culture.[5] In addition to promoting her agenda of environmental conservation, she linked the plight of the Appalachian environment with the plight of the Appalachian people. Her account of Appalachian life opens with a majestic description of her homeland in the mountains as a nature that is splendid in its beauty but one that is also "not easily tamed" and that must be "won" through hard work and dedication. She depicts scenes of church services that are held in an unadorned building, a preacher who speaks in simple language, and children who are baptized in the pond.

Emma also connects nature with domestic life by explaining that most domestic chores take place outside; her sketches of mountain life include chopping wood, growing vegetables, and taking care of livestock. Those chores that took place in the home such as sewing, weaving, cleaning, and cooking were taken to the porch when possible or done in a home where the door was always open. Once she establishes how fundamental the environment is to both their spiritual and domestic life, she demonstrates the ways in which the influx of urban tourists and capitalists are destroying that environment and culture. She expresses disgust over the useless paving of roads and destruction of the environment when hotels and factories are built in the mountains. She is also deeply saddened when locals are forced to earn a living as hotel workers and mill laborers, noting that this diminishes Appalachian skill sets, such as basket weaving. By the end of her novel, she is able to both depict the majestic life of the mountain people and instill a sense of guilt in the typically urban audience in an attempt to motivate them to protect this unique culture.

In addition to her fiction works, Emma wrote articles for the local paper and lectured in the surrounding area on similar subjects. She also enjoyed great friendships with many other female writers, artists, and speakers in the area.[6]

Sadly, for the young activist and author, by 1916 she was experiencing declining health again. This time the prognosis was serious—tuberculosis. Her doctors remained hopeful, claiming that she may recover with proper care and treatment, but Emma was doubtful. She wrote, "I do not think this doctor or anyone else has any idea how much I have been through in the past years or how worn out I am."[7] Her life had become increasingly difficult. Her marital problems had grown worse, resulting in bouts of separation from Frank, and her declining health affected her ability to earn money for the family. Although aware that she may never recover from this latest illness, Emma remained steadfast in her passion, writing about Appalachian life. In the final years of her life, Emma completed her last work, *Our Southern Birds* (1919), which documents the birds of the Walden's Ridge area.

On March 19, 1919, surrounded by Frank and her children, Emma Bell Miles died of tuberculosis. She left behind many admirers and a body of work that poignantly and beautifully depicts, glorifies, and defends Appalachia and its people.

NOTES

[1] Kay Baker Gaston, *Emma Bell Miles* (Signal Mountain, TN: Walden's Ridge Historical Association, 1985).

[2] Emma Bell Miles, Letter to Anna Ricketson, October 24, 1907, Unpublished Letters to Anna Ricketson (Chattanooga: Hamilton County Bicentennial Library).

[3] Ibid.

[4] Emma Bell Miles, Letter to Abby Crawford Milton, August 4, 1918, Abby Crawford Milton Collection of the Writings of Emma Bell Miles, 1918-1930 (Nashville: Tennessee State Library and Archives).

[5] Emma Bell Miles, *The Spirit of the Mountains* (New York: James Pott and Company, 1905).

[6] Emma had friendships with sisters Alice McGowan and Grace McGowan Cooke of the Chattanooga area, who both wrote for *Harper's Monthly*. Grace, like Emma, was concerned with the plight of Appalachia and its people,

particularly its women, and published her book, *The Power and the Glory: An Appalachian Novel* (1910) on that topic. Elizabeth Engelhardt writes about their friendship and writing careers in her book *The Tangled Roots of Feminism, Environmentalism, and Appalachian Literature* (2003).

[7] Miles, letter to Anna Ricketson.

FOUR PROMINENT TENNESSEE SUFFRAGISTS

Tennessee's Superb Suffragists

PAULA F. CASEY

The story of the Nineteenth Amendment's passage is one of the greatest in American history. Those who struggled for seventy-two years to include women in the US Constitution achieved their goal through a peaceful revolution without firing a single shot or shedding one drop of human blood.

However, ratification was obtained only after hundreds of campaigns in state after state as the suffragists met with defeat. Few know that it was women seeking the vote who first picketed the White House for a political cause or that these courageous women faced jail, hunger strikes, and forced feedings. Years of organizing, ridicule, and great disappointment followed the Civil War when the Fourteenth and Fifteenth Amendments excluded women from voting. Yet they persevered until achieving victory in Nashville on August 18, 1920.

Tennessee became known as "The Perfect 36" — the last state that could possibly ratify the Nineteenth Amendment and make it law. No other state was even close. When the Nineteenth Amendment finally passed Congress on June 4, 1919, the battleground shifted to the states, where thirty-six of the then forty-eight states were needed for ratification. By the summer of 1920, thirty-five states had ratified and eight had rejected it. With no other state close to ratifying, the pro-suffrage forces looked to Tennessee.

How did Tennessee, a border state with no history of progressivism, become significant? The answer was all the dedicated Tennesseans who believed deeply in the cause and organized brilliantly across the state in the face of unyielding opposition.

In the play, *Tennessee Women for the Vote: A Woman Suffrage Rally, 1913* by B. Ayne Cantrell, you will read about four prominent Tennessee suffragists. These women were remarkable because they assumed leadership roles in a time when women were not welcomed as leaders. They led the battle for hearts and minds and against prevailing social customs.

MARTHA ELIZABETH MOORE ALLEN OF MEMPHIS
1849–1936

A pioneering suffragist, Allen was a member of the Memphis Equal Suffrage Association, served as president of Memphis Equal Suffrage League from 1906–1912, and was active in the National American Woman Suffrage Association (NAWSA). Her dedication to woman suffrage began during the 1870s when she saw Susan B. Anthony speak at a rally. She was living with her father-in-law at the time and he did not support woman suffrage, so she did not fully engage in suffrage activities until 1889 when she and her husband moved from Indiana to Nashville.

In 1898, they relocated to Memphis. Allen promptly joined an Equal Suffrage Association when it originated there in 1904. It failed due to lack of funds. This was not the end of her involvement with suffrage. She became the founding president of a small group called the Equal Suffrage League in 1906. She served as president until 1912.

During this time, she worked to organize throughout the state. These efforts included countless parades, rallies, flying of flags, and rummage sales. Her efforts paid off and she earned the honor of being called the grandmother of the Memphis League of Women Voters. An eloquent orator, she issued press releases and led a successful campaign for admission of women to the Memphis Law School.

Allen served as a delegate to three Women's Christian Temperance Union (WCTU) and two national suffrage conventions. A Christian Scientist, she authored a pamphlet entitled "Rambles with Christian Endeavors" as well as numerous articles on temperance and suffrage. She listed her recreations as "driving through parks, country rambles" and was a member of the Nineteenth Century Club, Civic League, Ladies' Hermitage Association, WCTU, Daughters of 1812, and Daughters of the American Revolution. In her last years, she eventually retired from public life due to illness and died at the age of eighty-seven.[1]

ANNE DALLAS DUDLEY OF NASHVILLE

1876–1955

Courtesy of the Tennessee State
Library and Archives

Anne Dallas Dudley and Two Children

One of Tennessee's most influential suffragists, Dudley founded the Nashville Equal Suffrage League, served as president of the Tennessee Equal Suffrage League in 1915, and became vice president of NAWSA in 1917. She was an indispensable campaigner for the final ratification effort in 1920.

Her beauty, charm, and eloquence made her the living refutation of the derogatory "she-male" label often attributed to suffragists by opponents. Her political acumen was widely recognized. She once demolished an anti-suffragist's argument that "because only men bear arms, only men should vote." Dudley pithily replied, "Yes, but women bear armies."[2]

Dudley and several other women met in the Tulane Hotel's back parlor in September 1911 to found the Nashville Equal Suffrage League. The organization was dedicated to building local support while "quietly and earnestly avoiding militant methods." The elegant Dudley served as the organization's first president. During her presidency, the League organized giant "May Day" suffrage parades usually led by Dudley and her children.[3] Dudley also helped bring the National Suffrage Convention to Nashville in 1914, which was one of the largest conventions ever held there.

Dudley was elected to head the Tennessee Equal Suffrage Association in 1915 after serving in the local league for four years. She helped to introduce and lobbied for a suffrage amendment to the state constitution. Although the amendment was defeated, the legislature later passed partial suffrage legislation in 1919 to grant women the right to vote in presidential and municipal elections.

Dudley contributed significantly on the national suffrage stage in 1917 to advancing legislation when she became third vice president of the NAWSA. Along with Catherine Talty Kenny and Abby Crawford Milton, she led the campaign to approve ratification when the time came for Tennessee's pivotal vote in 1920.

Her legacy has been recognized in several ways:

- Featured in the Tennessee Woman Suffrage Memorial in Knoxville with Lizzie Crozier French of Knoxville and Elizabeth Avery Meriwether of Memphis
- Featured with ten other prominent Tennesseans in *The Pride of Tennessee*, the official Tennessee State Bicentennial Portrait which hangs in the Tennessee State Capitol

- Recognized with a historical marker in Nashville's Centennial Park
- Inducted into the National Women's Hall of Fame in 1995 in Seneca Falls, New York.[4]

LIDE SMITH MERIWETHER OF MEMPHIS

1829–1913

Image courtesy of Bryn Mawr College
Special Collection

Lide Smith Meriwether

Lide Smith Meriwether began her activism on behalf of women in 1872 with the publication of *Soundings,* a periodical dedicated to bringing respectable women to the rescue of prostitutes, whom she depicted as victims rather than moral untouchables. She campaigned vigorously for prohibition of liquor, for raising the legal age of consent for sexual activity and marriage, for a police matron to search and otherwise deal with women in Memphis, and most notably for woman suffrage.

Alongside her crusading sister-in-law, Elizabeth Avery Meriwether, the first woman in Tennessee to champion voting rights for women, Lide Meriwether used the temperance issue to advance the suffrage cause. In 1886, NAWSA hired her to organize the state, which resulted in fledgling Equal Rights Clubs in Nashville, Knoxville, Jackson, Greeneville, and Murfreesboro.

She urged the editor of *The Memphis Appeal* to publish its first pro-suffrage editorial on July 29, 1888, stating, "Intelligent people realize the injustice of withholding the ballot from women." A founder and president of Tennessee's first Equal Suffrage Society in Memphis in 1889, Meriwether succeeded Elizabeth Lisle Saxon as president of the Tennessee Woman Suffrage Association and was given the honorary title "President for Life" in 1900.[5]

In her suffrage petition of 1895, Meriwether outlined reasons for Tennessee women to demand suffrage. At that time, under the law, women had the same rights as minors, aliens, paupers, criminals, and idiots. In her petition, she passionately argued against this indiscriminate classification. She demanded that married women gain the right to own their clothing, their property, and wages. She submitted that women should have the right to gain custody of their own children. She sent this "confession of faith" to the president of every suffrage club and WCTU in Tennessee, allowing a fortnight to obtain signatures. In two weeks, it was returned with the names of 535 women, while several presidents wrote, "If you could only give us two weeks more, we could double the number."[6]

Meriwether proudly wore a yellow ribbon as a suffrage badge symbolizing justice through political equality. Her crusading activism paved the road to suffrage victory.

SUE SHELTON WHITE OF JACKSON

1887–1943

Prints and Photographs Division,
Library of Congress, Washington, DC

Sue Shelton White

One of Tennessee's most effective suffragists, White was one of the first women court reporters in the state in 1907. She joined the woman suffrage movement and helped organize the Jackson Equal Suffrage League in 1911. While working to increase support for suffrage in Tennessee, she served as recording secretary for the Tennessee Equal Suffrage Association beginning in 1913. She later came to believe that the policies and methods of the activist National Woman's Party (NWP) were more effective and changed her allegiance in 1918.

Upon moving to Washington, DC, White became Tennessee chair of the NWP in 1918 and edited the organization's newspaper, *The Suffragist.* She achieved additional notoriety for participating in a suffrage demonstration in which the NWP burned President Woodrow Wilson in effigy. Arrested for picketing the White House in 1919, she served five days in the Old Work House, a condemned jail. After her release, White joined the "Prison Special," a chartered railroad car that traveled around the country bringing the suffrage issue to the people. She was the only known Tennessee woman jailed for her suffrage work.

During the 1920 ratification campaign in Nashville, she headed the NWP campaign and coordinated their work with Carrie Chapman Catt's NAWSA as both lobbied lawmakers. Known for being politically sagacious, "Miss Sue" coordinated her workers out of the Tulane Hotel. Catt's group operated from the Hermitage Hotel.

In 1923, after the amendment was passed, White earned her law degree from Washington College of Law in Washington, DC, and worked for Senator Kenneth McKellar (D–TN). She later worked as an attorney for Franklin Roosevelt's administration to help implement the Social Security Act. In the 1920s–1930s, she held other important posts in Washington, DC, with the Democratic National

Committee, the Woman's Bureau, and the Social Security Board. After a long bout with cancer, White died on May 6, 1943.[7]

After the suffragists' years of hard work, the struggle culminated in Tennessee. In an article entitled "Armageddon in Tennessee," Anastatia Sims wrote, "If the suffragists could win the approval of just one more state, they would, at long last, achieve their goal. When the Delaware legislature unexpectedly defeated the amendment in early June, women pinned their hopes on Tennessee. During a steamy Southern summer, Nashville, the 'Athens of the South,' became the site of one of the most fiercely fought contests in American political history. For the amendment's friends and foes alike, it was Armageddon—the final battle in the long, bitter struggle . . ."[8]

The pressure began for Governor A. H. Roberts to call a special session. On June 19, Sue Shelton White sent Roberts a letter requesting a special session. Other prominent Tennesseans requested that the governor call a special session so women could vote in the August 5 state primary. The opposition was so fierce that Roberts did not call the special session until August 9 after his party's primary.

The Tennessee Senate voted 25–4 in favor of the amendment on August 13. The seventy-two-year struggle had come down to one last vote in the Tennessee House of Representatives.

Debate began on Wednesday, August 18. After numerous parliamentary maneuverings and the surprising favorable vote cast by Representative Harry Burn of Niota, the final vote was 49–47. Despite several challenges to Tennessee's ratification, the vote held and American women were eligible to vote in the 1920 presidential election. This remarkable story is more fully told in *The Perfect 36: Tennessee Delivers Woman Suffrage,* which was donated to every school, library, and college in the state of Tennessee.[9]

Notes

[1] J. B. Mann Suffrage Collection, "Martha Moore Allen," Memphis Public Library and Information Center-Memphis Room.

2 Carol Lynn Yellin and Janann Sherman, *The Perfect 36: Tennessee Delivers Woman Suffrage* (Oak Ridge: Iris Press, 1998), 84.

3 Ibid., 53–54.

4 Anne Dallas Dudley, http://www.hmdb.org/Marker.asp?Marker=4524, Accessed June 2012.

[5] *MemphisHistory.com,* http://memphishistory.com/People/TheActivists/LideSmithMeriwether.aspx.

[6] Susan B. Anthony and Ida Husted Harper, *History of Woman Suffrage* 4 (Salem, NH: Ayer Company Publishing Inc., Reprint Edition 1985), 927–928.

[7] Yellin and Sherman, 56.

[8] Anastatia Sims, "Armageddon in Tennessee: The Final Battle Over the 19th Amendment" in *One Woman, One Vote: Rediscovering the Woman Suffrage Movement* (Troutdale, OR: NewSage Press, 1995), 346–347.

[9] *The Perfect 36: Tennessee Delivers Woman Suffrage,* http://www.theperfect36.com.

A Play in One Act

Tennessee Women for the Vote:
A Woman Suffrage Rally, 1913

B. Ayne Cantrell

Courtesy of the Tennessee State Library and Archives

Marching Suffragists

Program Note: *The rally is set in Murfreesboro, Tennessee, 1913. While all the suffragists are women from Tennessee history, their coming together at this time and place is completely imaginary. Portions of their speeches are authentic, but much has been rearranged, and the historical period has been condensed for dramatic effect. Lide Meriwether, for example, retired from the struggle for woman's vote in 1900 after she had been the driving force for the movement in Tennessee for over twenty years.[1] White, Allen, and Dudley made their contributions to the campaign several years later.*

A podium stands center stage with two straight chairs at stage left and two straight chairs at stage right. These are flanked by yellow banners, which read, "VOTES FOR WOMEN!" Another podium and chair are stationed at stage right. The narrator enters and sits stage right behind the podium.

Wearing yellow suffrage sashes and period costumes, speakers White, Meriwether, Allen, and Dudley march into the hall and down to stage left carrying signs and chanting slogans: "Women's votes are women's rights!" "No more tyranny!" "We demand the vote!" "Women are men's equal!" "Give us the vote!" These women are trailed by audience supporters. Among the spectators are a number of men and women opposed to suffrage for women. These are the "hecklers" of the script. They are vocal in their opposition and voice protests more often than the text allows. Likewise, although the script does not give them speeches, spectators in favor of suffrage for women are encouraged to voice their support throughout the rally.

When the speakers reach the stage, they take their seats SR of the podium (White and Meriwether) and SL of the podium (Allen and Dudley). Their supporters take seats in the audience. When all are seated, the narrator rises and goes to the podium to introduce the rally.

The Narrator enters stage right and stands at the podium to introduce the rally.

NARRATOR: Today we ask you to go back in time to the year 1913, when women all across Tennessee were campaigning for woman's suffrage. These suffragists participated in marches similar to the one staged here today; they gave speeches and engaged in debates; they distributed leaflets in support of woman's suffrage; they set up booths at fairs and sold buttons to raise money for their campaign; they wrote editorials and letters. They were political activists at a time in American history when it was thought that a woman's place was in the home. By 1913, a permanent statewide suffrage organization, the Tennessee Equal Suffrage Association, was active in the state along with suffrage societies in Knoxville, Nashville, Morristown, Chattanooga, and Jackson.[2]

By and large, the Tennessee campaign for woman's suffrage was not a militant one. In fact, Tennessee suffragists often voiced protests against militancy, arguing that practices such as picketing the White House were "unworthy of southern women."[3] Nonetheless, we have with us this evening a true militant heroine on the behalf of women—Sue Shelton White of Jackson, Tennessee, who has the distinction of being the only Tennessee woman to be arrested and jailed because of her suffrage work.[4] Just recently Miss White was elected recording secretary of the Tennessee Equal Suffrage Association.[5] She will now open our demonstration for woman suffrage with a few remarks about the history of the movement.

As the narrator returns to her seat at SR, Sue White approaches the podium but is interrupted before she begins her speech.

HECKLER 1: Go back home, Sue. We don't want your kind in Murfreesboro!

WHITE: Sir, I will *not* go home until every woman in Tennessee and in the United States has the vote. Should not all who are governed by the law, and that includes women, have a voice in making the law? We women have too long been denied this right. The common law of England, which also is the law of the United States, says women are inferior to men.[6] We women are classed with children, criminals, and the mentally insane. If we are married, we cannot own property, and if we work outside the home, our earnings belong to our husbands. In fact, everything we have — our clothes and other personal possessions, even our children — belongs to our husbands. And should our husbands elect to beat us, the law allows it. Women (whether married or single) are not permitted to vote, to hold office, to serve on juries or otherwise participate in public affairs. Furthermore, we do not have easy access to higher education, and thereby we are limited to menial occupations. No, sir, I will *not* go home. I will *not* turn back until all these wrongs are rectified.

And I will not go home, sir, because women before me did not go home. In July 1848, an equal rights convention was held in Seneca Falls, New York, to discuss the rights of women. Convention attendees resolved that "woman is man's equal — was intended to be so by the Creator, and the highest good of the race demands that she should be recognized as such."[7] The convention's *Declaration of Sentiments* acknowledged, "The history of mankind is a history of repeated injuries and usurpations on the part of man toward woman, having in direct object the establishment of an absolute tyranny over her." In response to this tyranny, the women of the Seneca Falls convention resolved that it was the "duty of the women of this country to secure to themselves their sacred right of the elective franchise." But now in 1913 — sixty-five years later — we women still do not enjoy the right of the ballot box.

We southern women have lagged behind our northern sisters in the movement to win the right to vote, but Tennessee can be proud that we have taken a more active part among the southern states in this crusade.[8] Present with me on the platform are Tennessee women who have worked for woman suffrage. Among them is Mrs. Lide S. Meriwether of Memphis. Mrs. Meriwether has served as president of the first woman suffrage league in Tennessee, which was organized in Memphis in May 1889.[9] Since Mrs. Meriwether is one of the chief representatives of liberal thought in Tennessee, we have asked her to share with us her reasons for favoring the enfranchisement of women. I give you Mrs. Lide Meriwether.

Mrs. Meriwether comes forward and shakes Miss White's hand. Miss White retires to her seat.

MERIWETHER: I have often been asked why I am a suffragist, not only by men but also by women who have yet to join the crusade. Perhaps, there are some among you who are undecided.

HECKLER 2:   That's for sure. Why do you women want to vote?

MERIWETHER: We women want the right to vote, Sir, because "Being twenty-one years old, we object to being classed with minors. Born in America and loyal to her institutions, we protest against being made perpetual aliens. Costing the treasuries of our country nothing, we protest against acknowledging the male pauper as our political superior. Being obedient to law, we protest against the statute which classes us with the convict and makes the pardoned criminal our political superior. Being sane, we object to being classed with lunatics. Possessing an average amount of intelligence, we protest against legal classification with the idiot. We taxpayers claim the right to representation. We married women want to own our clothes. We married breadwinners want to own our earnings. We mothers want an equal partnership in our children. We educated women want the power to offset the illiterate vote in our state."[10]

These are the reasons I am a suffragist. The yellow ribbon I wear is my suffrage badge. I wear it proudly—as some of you do—because it stands for justice through political equality.[11] As one of the nationally recognized promoters of equal rights for women, Susan B. Anthony, told us when she visited Nashville, we "cannot rest until woman's name stands for as much as a man's name, until a woman's opinion is worth as much as a man's, and that means the ballot."[12] Women must be granted the liberty to vote and to enter politics—if they choose—only then will we be true citizens of Tennessee and of the United States. Thank you.

WHITE: Thank you, Mrs. Meriwether. Also among our platform guests is another leading suffragist from Memphis. Mrs. Jacob D. Allen served as president of the Tennessee Equal Suffrage Association from its inception in 1906 until 1912. She is also active in the National American Woman Suffrage Association.[13] Mrs. Allen—

ALLEN: Thank you, Miss White. Mrs. Meriwether alluded to the fact that there may be some among you who have not joined our cause. I think it most appropriate that my remarks be addressed to you.

HECKLER 2: It ain't gonna do no good!

ALLEN: I intend to try anyway, Madame. One of the most important functions of the Tennessee Equal Suffrage Association has been to place woman suffrage literature before the public. "We have tried novel ways of distributing our leaflets. We visit railway depots and place them in the timetable holders. We often mingle among crowds formed by some parade or collected by some unusual occurrence and hand out leaflets."[14] Today members of the association have been passing among you with pamphlets that I hope you will read. Without public support, we will not win the right to vote. We believe that if people understand the need for woman suffrage, they will favor it. Therefore, we have distributed thousands of leaflets and booklets across the state to educate our citizens on the importance of woman suffrage. One of the most popular pieces of literature that is distributed is entitled *Perhaps*, written by Carrie Chapman Catt, a leader of the national woman suffrage movement.

I now would like to read a portion of Mrs. Catt's remarks. She says, "Perhaps if you realized that the law guarantees or restricts your own personal liberty; protects or jeopardizes your health, your home, your happiness; regulates the food you eat, the clothes you wear, the books you read, the amusements you enjoy; in fact permits or prohibits your every act, you would feel a serious obligation to inquire into the nature of such authority over you. Perhaps if you knew that the booksellers of Denver reported that they had sold more books on civil government and political economy in six months after women were enfranchised in that state than in ten years before, you would be convinced that women appreciate the responsibility of voting, and prepare themselves to 'administer the sacrament of citizenship' intelligently. Perhaps if you knew the overwhelming testimony from the most prominent, responsible, and respected citizens of the suffrage states agrees that woman suffrage has resulted in better candidates for office, cleaner polling places, quieter elections, and improved legislation, and that women have grown more intelligent, self-reliant, respected, and womanly under its influence, you would feel it your duty to work that such results might come to all states."[15] A number of Tennessee women have taken up this challenge by Mrs. Catt. We have sent a petition to Congress along with over four hundred letters in favor of the proposed woman suffrage amendment to the Constitution of the United States.[16] We invite you citizens of Murfreesboro to join those of Kingston, Knoxville, Memphis, Nashville, Chattanooga, Jackson, and Morristown in our equal suffrage campaign.

HECKLER 3: Not all women want to vote, Mrs. Allen.

HECKLER 4: Allowing women to vote will take them away from their families. What are their children supposed to do without mothers?

HECKLER 5: Yes, that's right. If they get to vote, women will neglect their homes.

During these speeches, Dudley rises from her seat, goes up to Allen at the podium, and offers to respond to the hecklers.

DUDLEY: If I may, Mrs. Allen, I would like to speak to these objections commonly advanced against suffrage for women.

ALLEN: I will yield to Mrs. Guilford Dudley, who is one of the most influential suffragists in Tennessee. Most recently, in 1911, she founded the Nashville Suffrage League.[17] Welcome, Mrs. Dudley.

Allen returns to her seat.

DUDLEY: To those who believe that we should not allow women to vote because not all women want to vote, I ask, "Is that a just reason why those who need the ballot for their own protection should not have it? The ballot is not compulsory and those who wish to sit among the ashes of an old ideal while the Phoenix of the new is winging its way toward the dawn will still have the freedom of their will."[18] To those who are against woman suffrage because it will take women "out of the home," let me first state the obvious and that is that many women work outside the home. Secondly, the assumption that "all women have comfortable, attractive homes over which they have absolute jurisdiction" is false. Moreover, the modern woman needs the ballot to protect her home: "In days gone by she was not obligated to ask a city government to see that her water supply was pure. . . . She was not obligated to ask a corrupt city council for milk inspectors in order to see that her children were not infected with typhoid or tuberculosis." To those that say that woman will neglect her home for politics, I say, such a woman who would neglect her home for politics will probably neglect it for "bridge or something equally less vital." I predict that "the cradle will be rocked, the dishes washed, and still by feminine hands, even if women should give thirty minutes of their time a year for casting a vote."

HECKLER 1:   Women don't have time to vote anyway, Mrs. Dudley.

DUDLEY: "This objection is constantly advanced by some woman who has all the time in the world to have her hair curled and her nails manicured, her gowns fitted, and [who] thinks the giving of a pink tea one of the serious things in life." Give us the opportunity to take politics seriously. Give us the vote, and we will find the time to vote.

HECKLER 2:   We don't want our southern women to stain their hands with the dirty business of politics.

HECKLER 3:   Yes, that's right. Way to go, Jim. *All hecklers agree.*

DUDLEY: I have heard that objection before—the southern woman is too ladylike, too delicate to venture into the filthy atmosphere of the polling place. I say give her the vote, and she will clean up the polling place! The southern woman will not "hesitate to walk up to the ballot box to vote for some measure to protect her home and children or for the protection of some little laborer or other less fortunate woman."

   In closing, please allow me to say, "I have never yet met a man or woman who denied that taxation without representation is tyranny. I have never yet seen one who was such a traitor to our form of government that he did not believe that the government rests upon the consent of the governed. This is a government of, for, and by the people, and only the law denies that women are people. . . . In view of all these facts, it is not surprising that the demand for the woman's ballot increases hourly and that all the states are swinging jubilantly into line." As yet, you citizens of Murfreesboro do not have a woman suffrage league. It is our extreme hope that you will call upon your consciences and that you will join with us in this just cause. Women's Votes are Women's Rights! Thank you.

Dudley returns to her chair. The narrator comes to the podium at stage right.

NARRATOR: Mrs. Dudley, your call for the organization of a local woman suffrage league here in Murfreesboro did not go unheeded. In fact, in just one year—1914—Murfreesboro had its own suffrage league, and suffrage societies were formed in Clarksville, Franklin, and Gallatin as well.[19]

In 1920, Tennessee won national acclaim when it became the thirty-sixth state to ratify the Nineteenth Amendment of the Constitution of the United States. American women had finally earned the vote.

Women won the right to vote in this country only after a long struggle and much campaigning and crusading by women such as Sue Shelton White of Jackson *(White stands)*, Lide S. Meriwether of Memphis *(Meriwether stands)*, Martha Moore Allen of Memphis *(Allen stands)*, and Anne Dallas Dudley of Nashville *(Dudley stands)*. Today, you have been part of that history. Let us close with the words of Sue White who defined her philosophy toward women's rights six years after women won the vote. In 1926 in a speech to the Jackson Business & Professional Women's Club, she said —

WHITE: "We must remember the past, hold fast to the present, and build for the future. If you stand in our accepted place today, it is because some woman had to fight yesterday. We should be ashamed to stand on ground won by women in the past without making an effort to honor them by winning a higher and wider field for the future. It is a debt we owe."[20]

White begins singing the following popular suffrage song to the tune of "America." The other speakers come to the front of the stage right and left of White and join in singing:

> My country 'tis of thee
> To make your women free
> This is our plea.
> High have our hopes been raised
> In these enlightened days
> That for her justice praised
> Our land might be
> My native country thee
> Grant us equality!
> Then we shall see
> In this fair land of light
> Justice and truth and right
> Ruling instead of might
> Trust liberty.[21]

The speakers invite the audience to sing, and the rally concludes as the speakers begin the song again and march off stage left.

Notes

1 Anastatia Sims, "Woman Suffrage Movement," *The Tennessee Encyclopedia of History and Culture,* Version 2.0, accessed May 25, 2012, http://tennesseeencyclopedia.net/entry.php?rec=1528/.

2 A. Elizabeth Taylor, "Tennessee: The Thirty-Sixth State," in *Votes for Women! The Woman Suffrage Movement in Tennessee, the South, and the Nation,* ed. Marjorie Spruill Wheeler (Knoxville: University of Tennessee Press, 1955), 54.

3 A. Elizabeth Taylor, *The Woman Suffrage Movement in Tennessee* (New York: Bookman Associates, 1957), 56.

4 Susan Sawyer, *More than Petticoats: Remarkable Tennessee Women* (Helena, Montana: Falcon Publishing, 2000), 100. White and other members of the National Woman's Party burned President Woodrow Wilson in effigy in front of the White House for his indifference to woman suffrage. They were arrested, convicted, and imprisoned for five days.

5 Ibid., 102.

6 White's outline of the law's subjection of women is taken from Taylor, *The Woman Suffrage Movement in Tennessee,* 11–12.

7 Quotations from the Seneca Falls convention are excerpted from "Declaration of Sentiments and Resolutions of the Woman's Rights Convention, Held at Seneca Falls, 19–20 July 1848," *The Selected Papers of Elizabeth Cady Stanton & Susan B. Anthony,* vol. 1 (New Brunswick, N. J.: Rutgers University Press, 1997), The Elizabeth Cady Stanton & Susan B. Anthony Papers Project, accessed May 27, 2012, http://ecssba.rutgers.edu/docs/seneca.html/.

8 Taylor, *The Suffrage Movement in Tennessee,* 15.

9 Taylor, "Tennessee: The Thirty-Sixth State," 52.

10 "Tennessee," *History of Woman Suffrage,* Vol. IV, eds. Elizabeth Cady Stanton, Susan B. Anthony, Matilda Joslyn Gage, and Ida H. Harper (New York, 1881-1922), 927–928, quoted in Project Gutenberg EBook #29870, Chapter LXIV (31 August 2009). http://www.gutenberg.org/files/29870/29870-h/29870-h.htm#CHAPTER_LXIV.

11 Yellow was chosen as the emblematic color for the national woman suffrage movement after Kansas suffragists adopted the state symbol of the sunflower for a campaign in 1867. Printed on the sashes was "Votes for

Women." "Treasures of American History: Woman Suffrage," Smithsonian National Museum of American History, accessed May 21, 2012, http:// americanhistory.si.edu/exhibitions/small_exhibition.cfm?key=1267&exk ey=143&pagekey=242/.

[12] Nashville *American*, October 27, 1897, quoted in Taylor, *The Suffrage Movement in Tennessee*, 22. Anthony was in Nashville in October 1897 to attend the convention of the National Council of Women of the United States.

[13] "Heroines of Tennessee: A Suffrage Roll of Honor," *History's Women: An Online Magazine*, accessed May 26, 2012, http://www.historyswomen. com/admire/Admire39.html/.

[14] Report of the Tennessee Equal Suffrage Association, 1910, quoted in Taylor, *The Suffrage Movement in Tennessee*, 31.

[15] Memphis *Commercial Appeal*, October 20, 1909, quoted in Taylor, *The Suffrage Movement in Tennessee*, 30.

[16] Taylor, *The Suffrage Movement in Tennessee*, 32.

[17] "Heroines of Tennessee."

[18] Dudley's speech is excerpted from an address she gave to the Nashville Housekeeper's Club, Nashville *Tennessean*, February 20, 1913, quoted in Taylor, *The Suffrage Movement in Tennessee*, 41–43.

[19] Taylor, *The Suffrage Movement in Tennessee*, 36.

[20] Quoted in Sawyer, *More than Petticoats*, 107.

[21] Memphis *News Scimitar*, May 4, 1914, quoted in Taylor, *The Suffrage Movement in Tennessee*, 132.

BRENDA VINEYARD RUNYON

1866-1929

The Nation's First Woman's Bank

TAYLOR EMERY

Courtesy of the Tennessee State Library and Archives

Brenda Vineyard Runyon

The town of Liberty, Missouri, was an apt location for the first woman banker to make her initial appearance. Born there in 1866 to Benjamin W. and Nancy Preston Vineyard, Brenda Mary Vineyard moved to Kentucky where her parents became noted educators. She spent most of her youth there and attended her parents' school. As a daughter of educators, she was in a position to marry a learned man, which she did when she wed Dr. Frank Jasper Runyon of Trenton, Kentucky, in his hometown in 1885. The new family moved across the state line to Clarksville, Tennessee, in 1887.[1] Once established in their new locale, Runyon exemplified her role of the wife of a prominent physician and mother of two sons by becoming involved in numerous endeavors through her associations with influential business and civic-minded people.

As the wife of a physician in Clarksville at the turn of the twentieth century, Brenda Vineyard Runyon devoted much of her time to her husband and two sons. She participated in local civic and social activities, which included helping to establish a public library, a city-county hospital, the local chapter of the American Red Cross and American War Mothers, along with other activities. With each accomplishment, she had a desire to do more for her community. At age fifty and with her past volunteer successes, she acted on advice from a family friend and local banker, Sterling Fort, as to what she should attempt next. He suggested that she open a bank run entirely by women: "I told him I knew nothing about banking except how to compute interest. He suggested that I could learn."[2] And so began her next challenge.

She approached Mrs. J. E. Elder to serve as vice president, who reluctantly accepted. She then chose Mrs. M. G. Lyle as secretary/cashier. Keeping the proposal secret, Runyon and Lyle traveled to Kentucky to learn about banking. Runyon "was soon informed that Mrs. Lyle was making herself such an efficient cashier" that the Kentucky bank president might attempt to hire her himself. However, Runyon had no doubt that Lyle would remain with her as Lyle's "home and interests [were] in Clarksville." The secrecy was intended to demonstrate the women's discretion. "They [the account holders] are now assured that we can keep our affairs to ourselves, which proves to them that theirs, too, will be taken care of in a like manner when we come to handle them," Runyon explained to Vonnie Rector Griffith of the *Ladies' Home Journal*.[3]

On October 6, 1919, the bank opened for business in the Montgomery Hotel. The local newspaper, *The Leaf Chronicle*, reported the opening "was greeted by a deluge of customers, many of whom had been waiting in line for the distinction of being the first depositor in the First Woman's Bank of Tennessee. Mrs. Luia B. Epperson . . . ha[d] that distinction." Throughout the day, the bank stayed busy, and by "2 o'clock [the deposits] amounted to $20,058.75, representing . . . over seventy depositors." Runyon commemorated the opening by offering men "an El Sidelo cigar and [giving] ladies . . . beautiful dahlias."[4] On opening day, a competitor ran this advertisement: "Greetings: The First National Bank of Clarksville extends to The First Woman's Bank of Tennessee Best Wishes for a Career of Continuous Success and Usefulness."[5] A few days later, the bank ran its own advertisement:

Bobbie Burns said:
'Tis the saving
Not the getting.'
As soon as you get it
put it in the
First
Woman's

Bank
and not only save it, but
get 3% interest on it.
Savings and Checking
Accounts Solicited.[6]

Even though the bankers were female, Runyon did not consider the gender of the depositors and stockholders, but would not sell more than one or two shares to any one individual, which implied an egalitarian concept and prevented anyone from gaining controlling interest. During opening day, ten different shares of the Initial Public Offering (IPO) stock, with the stated value of $100.00 per share, sold before Runyon and Lyle issued the eleventh certificate to Hattie G. Carney, who purchased one share.[7] The bank performed so well that within fourteen months, it paid a small dividend to investors. In addition to Runyon and Elder, the bank's directors included seven other women.[8]

At the October 1919 American Bankers' Convention held in St. Louis, Missouri, Vonnie Rector Griffith interviewed Runyon for the *Ladies' Home Journal*. She noted Runyon was "a unique figure at the [meeting]" which suggested that she was the only banker of her gender present. Griffith also described her as "a woman of character and poise, who is interested in many problems that come up in her home town, where she has taken part in civic as well as social affairs." Runyon, however, did not think of herself as unique nor did she believe she was the first female president of a United States bank. She explained to Griffith:

No, I am not the first woman president of a bank . . . I have been told that there was at one time a bank in Joplin, Missouri, that had a woman as its president. But this bank,

I understand, had some men as directors and was absorbed by another bank, operated by men . . . [A] bank in Texas . . . once claimed a woman as its president. She inherited the bank from her husband; and at her death it was no longer run by a woman . . . [I]n Meridian, Mississippi, a woman has for many years been associated with her father in banking and insurance.[9]

The bank remained viable until 1926 when its founder suffered a serious injury. On April 28, 1926, during Better Homes Week, Runyon suffered a broken left hip. Her recuperation was arduous, "[spending] five months in a cast following an operation to correct her . . . injury," and with no one wanting to assume her role, the decision was made to merge her bank with another. Seventeen months later, Runyon fractured her left leg in an automobile wreck. This recovery was less strenuous than the first, and she was soon mobile. On February 2, 1929, she had been in town even though the weather was frigid and snowy. The next morning, February 3, 1929, unexpectedly, she died of "acute oedema (sic) of the lungs . . . a pulse and heart that . . . beat in perfect unison with the many activities of Clarksville were stilled,"[10] as an anonymous reporter wrote in the local paper. Although five inches of snow had fallen, people packed her funeral.

In 1975, forty-nine years after the First Woman's Bank of Tennessee officially closed, controversy erupted. During the height of the feminist movement, the First Woman's Bank of New York opened with claims of being the first bank in the nation run completely by women. Ironically, the bank opened for business almost fifty-six years to the date of the opening of the First Woman's Bank of Tennessee. News organizations picked up the story. Both Runyon's grandsons—Charles Runyon, Jr. and Frank J. Runyon III—set about to correct the misinformation. Charles contacted the editor of the *Leaf Chronicle*, who sent an Associated Press dispatch containing clarifications about the First Woman's Bank in Clarksville.[11] Frank wrote Madeline H. McWhinney, president of the New York bank, informing her of the bank's erroneous claim as the first bank run by women. McWhinney acknowledged her bank's mistake and acquiesced Runyon's bank was "the real First Woman's Bank. Our research was obviously not good . . . We will change the wording of our brochures to give credit where credit is due as soon as we can . . . [and] I hope even more that you will find us worthy successors to your grandmother's endeavors."[12]

However, McWhinney's promise did not change perception of the New York bank as the first woman's bank. The propaganda continued. Only *People* magazine acknowledged the *first* woman's bank in a cursory parenthetical comment within a 1975 article.[13] The New York bank did not prove to be "worthy successors to [Runyon's] endeavors." Only when United States citizens, including bankers, know the facts, can Brenda Vineyard Runyon's remarkable accomplishments be fully appreciated.

NOTES

[1] *Montgomery County Tennessee Family History Book 2000* (Paducah, KY: Turner Publishing, 2000), 285.

[2] Vonnie Rector Griffith, "The First Woman President of the First Woman's Bank in the United States." *Ladies' Home Journal*. June 1920.

[3] Ibid.

[4] "Clarksville's Newest Bank Opens." *Leaf Chronicle*. October 6, 1919, 3.

[5] First National Bank ad. *Leaf Chronicle*. October 6, 1919, 4.

[6] First Woman's Bank ad. *Leaf Chronicle*. October 15, 1919, 6.

[7] First Woman's Bank of Tennessee Stock Certificate. Photocopy. Tennessee State Library and Archives AC #76-148.

[8] Ursula Smith Beach. *Along the Warioto or a History of Montgomery County, Tennessee* (Nashville: McQuiddy Press, 1964), 323.

[9] Griffith, "The First Woman President of the First Woman's Bank in the United States." *Ladies' Home Journal.* June 1920.

[10] "Club and Business Leader Dies," *Leaf Chronicle.* February 4, 1929, 1.

[11] James Charlet, Jr. letter and attachment to Charles Runyon, Jr. November 26, 1975. Photocopy. Tennessee State Library and Archives AC#76-148.

[12] Madeline H. McWhinney letter to Frank J. Runyon. November 21, 1975. Photocopy. Tennessee State Library and Archives AC #76-148.

[13] Patricia Burstein, "Never Fear — Livia's Here! and the New Women's Bank Is Opening Its Doors." *People.* October 20, 1975. Vol. 4. No.16.

Emma Rochelle Wheeler

1882–1957

A Beacon of Light

Rita Lorraine Hubbard

*African Americans of Chattanooga:
A History of Unsung Heroes,*
by Rita Lorraine Hubbard

Emma Rochelle Wheeler

T hroughout history, women have handled households, influenced young minds, encouraged male counterparts, and generally made life better for those around them. While these are important accomplishments, some women have done even more, breaking barriers, gaining new ground, uplifting their own races, and inspiring their own communities — or entire nations — in the process.

Dr. Emma Rochelle Wheeler was one of those women. Born in 1882, Emma faced a stack of hurdles: She was black, she was female, and the children in her world topped out of school at eighth grade, *if* they went to school at all. Even worse, black women of her day were typically consigned to careers as nannies, cooks, and farm workers.

Emma's life might have been the same, except that her father enjoyed a slightly better living than other blacks in the area. As a self-taught veterinarian in rural Gainesville, Florida, his services were in high demand and his pay came in the form of fresh vegetables, dinner invitations, and sometimes, actual money. This prestige afforded his family more opportunities than most, even making it possible to take six-year-old Emma to a doctor when her eyes were bothering her.

Her physician was a woman! This was unheard of in 1888, and for Emma, it was love at first sight. Emma decided that if this woman could be a doctor, she could, too. The two formed a lasting friendship, and the woman encouraged Emma throughout the years.

Emma attended Cookman Institute[1] and received her first teaching certificate on August 13, 1893, at eleven years old! This may seem strange, but it was perfectly acceptable for young girls to teach in that day, though most were a few years older before they did. Emma's second certificate at age fourteen qualified her to teach third grade, but she did not officially became part of the state teachers association until February 1900. With that move, she cleared the earliest hurdles in her life, receiving a quality education and becoming a teacher instead of a cook or a laborer.

Soon afterward, Emma married fellow teacher Joseph R. Howard, and they were soon expecting their first child. Like countless wives before her, Emma put her life's dream aside and concentrated on being a good wife and mother. Unfortunately, tragedy struck when Joseph contracted typhoid fever and died without ever meeting his son, Joseph, Jr. Now Emma faced a new hurdle: transitioning from newlywed to new mother to widow, all in less than two years! But Emma was no quitter. With money her husband had put aside for her and help from her father, she picked up the pieces of her broken life and enrolled in Meharry Medical College in Nashville.

With the female doctor cheering her on and her baby in tow, Emma attended her first class on September 4, 1901. She studied chemistry, recited anatomy, and practiced medical procedures on life-sized papier-mâché models of the male and female body. She worked with sections of the kidney, models of the brain, and even learned to mix and prepare pharmaceutical drugs, because in her day, physicians often mixed their own drugs.

After four years of lab work and study, Emma cleared the next hurdle and became one of only five African American women to graduate from Meharry Medical College. That same week in 1905, she celebrated her twenty-third birthday, and married her new love, Dr. John N. Wheeler, who would be her main supporter at a time when women were expected to be anything except physicians.

Emma and John had a whirlwind honeymoon, and then settled in the bustling city of Chattanooga, Tennessee. Since area hospitals refused to admit black patients or the doctors who tended them, the Wheelers set up separate offices for their patients on Main Street. They could have worked in the same office, but Emma opted to attract her own clientele on the strength of her own unique skills, knowledge, and bedside manner.

With over thirteen thousand blacks in the city, the medical business was good. Still, Emma hated the fact that they had no hospital of their own. She began saving the money she earned for the day she could finally do something about it, and that day came ten years later in 1915. That was when Emma purchased two empty lots on East Eighth Street and drew up plans for a hospital. It must have a large surgical ward and separate rooms for new mothers, and it needed lots of space for her growing family, because Emma's home overflowed with children. She still had only one biological child, Joseph, Jr., but she happily adopted her niece and nephew and an adorable girl named Bette.[2] She also sponsored neighborhood children from all over the city, and this generosity of spirit earned her the Chattanooga NAACP title of "Negro Mother of The Year."

As the plans moved forward, Emma had only half of what it would cost to build her new hospital.[3] But this new hurdle didn't stop her. Her husband could have given her the rest, but she had long ago decided that her hospital, which she christened Walden, would be her own. She would plan, build, and manage it, and John's only role would be to offer encouragement on good days, and a sympathetic ear on the bad.

Walden Hospital was dedicated on July 30, 1915. The mayor, the city physician, and a host of male African American physicians attended the services and offered their blessing to Chattanooga's lone female African American physician.

Because of Emma's courage, determination, and foresight, blacks now had a hospital of their own; one they could hope in and be proud of. It had a bed capacity of thirty patients, which included nine private rooms with two beds in each, and one large ward with twelve beds. It also had surgical, maternity and nursery departments, and a house staff of two, with three nurses. For the first time, the black physicians and surgeons who patronized it enjoyed full admitting privileges and full charge of their patients. The average load was twelve patients per month.

Walden soon became known as the "beacon of light" for the community. It was so successful that Emma was able to pay the balance in full within three years of opening.[4] After ten years of operation, she transformed it into Chattanooga's first and only African American teaching hospital by starting a nurse training school for black students who dared to dream of becoming more than just housekeepers, janitors, and cooks.

Emma also started the Nurse Services Club, a unique "wellness" club she operated separately from Walden Hospital. Minorities and poorer citizens usually struggled to pay when hospitalization was necessary, but with Emma's plan, they could pay a fixed amount while they were well. This guaranteed two free weeks of hospitalization when the need arose, and at-home assistance by one of Emma's nurses upon discharge.[5] The price was twenty-five cents per week[6] and participation eventually grew to five hundred members.[7] Even the white hospitals did not have a club like this one!

Emma's success as a physician, visionary, and innovator brought many changes to Chattanooga. She helped the Chattanooga Street Car Company by servicing their black employees who were routinely denied admittance to white hospitals. Her open-door policy afforded physicians of every race the opportunity to practice and improve their medical knowledge and skills, and several white doctors with black patients took advantage of this opportunity. Walden Hospital even became a point of interest for the State of Tennessee in 1936, greatly improving tourism and luring high-profile visitors like Mary McLeod Bethune and Paul Robeson to tour the facilities when they were in town.

Emma's services stretched even further than her own community. During World War II, black men were sorely needed to help fight, but they needed a physical examination first. Even with this pressing need, area hospitals still refused admittance, so Emma did her part for the country by performing the exams herself.

Emma kept her hospital's doors open for thirty-eight years, but when the city opened a municipally owned black hospital and Emma's health began to fail, she finally closed her doors. She died at Hubbard Hospital on the Meharry Medical College campus on September 12, 1957. She was seventy-one.

Her body was returned to Chattanooga and interred in Highland Cemetery, and it is there that you'll find her gravestone. It is set apart and situated a little higher than the other stones, a sure sign that Emma remains a beacon of hope to the Chattanooga community.

NOTES

[1] Cookman was the first institution of higher education for Negroes ever established in Florida.

[2] Telephone and written interview by author with Bette Wheeler-Strictland of Chicago, Illinois.

[3] Ibid.

[4] "Walden Hospital to Close June 30." *Chattanooga Times* (Chattanooga: June 14, 1953).

[5] Ibid.

[6] Telephone interview by author with Josephine Wheeler, wife of George Wheeler, and daughter-in-law of Dr. Emma Rochelle Wheeler.

[7] "Dr. Wheeler Dies; Negro Physician," *Chattanooga Times* (Chattanooga: April 4, 1940).

EDITH O'KEEFE SUSONG

1890–1974

Wings on My Feet
MARGIE HUMPHREY LECOULTRE

Courtesy of *The Greeneville Sun*

Edith O'Keefe Susong

On October 1, 1966, on the fiftieth anniversary of the beginning of Edith O'Keefe Susong's career at the head of a community newspaper, she recalled her first full day on the job as a newspaperwoman, October 1, 1916. She wrote:

> I tripped down the two blocks to the location of my 'plant' with wings on my feet. I had a mortgage for $4,000 in my hand, but I also had a means of livelihood for my two children, and I was ready to go to work with a will. If I had realized how utterly impossible was the task that I was undertaking, I'd have turned at the door and fled. But since I had no comprehension of what I was trying to do, I breezed gaily in, greeted the two employees, and prepared to take over.[1]

Thus began the newspaper career of an extremely talented woman.

Edith O'Keefe was schooled by her mother until the ninth grade, when she went to what is now St. Catherine's School, in Richmond, Virginia. Later, she spent a short time at Agnes Scott College in Decatur, Georgia.

She returned to Greeneville to pursue a position in teaching, was hired, and was assigned to the Roby Fitzgerald School in 1909 and 1910. This was a fulfilling position for her, but she had met a handsome and promising graduate of the University of Virginia School of Law, and had fallen in love with him.

She and David Shields Susong were married on September 26, 1911; their wedding was a highlight of Greeneville's 1911 social season. He built her a house with his own hands while he practiced law. During this time, they became parents of two children: Alexander Elbert Susong and Martha Arnold Susong.

The marriage and the law practice were soon in trouble, however, because of Dave Susong's heavy drinking. One evening the owner of a small weekly newspaper in Greeneville, *The Greeneville Democrat*, saw that Dave was vulnerable because of his drinking and unloaded the failing newspaper on him in a card game.

Dave had to prevail upon a sister to sign a note to borrow money to run the newspaper he now owned. Edith didn't want her sister-in-law to sign the note, but years later, she said she didn't realize "that I was flying in the face of Providence and trying to prevent myself from having a means of livelihood."[2]

As time passed, he did not fulfill his part of the note bargain with his sister. Edith tried to help by writing occasional items, mostly social news, but her husband took no interest in the *Democrat*. Concerned for their jobs, the two employees encouraged her to take over the paper.

She had no background in newspaper publishing. However, she began to see that the paper might be her way to care for her children. She asked her sister-in-law to assign her husband's note to her, and she would take responsibility for it. Her sister-in-law agreed, and Edith became the owner of a newspaper that she had no idea how to run.

On October 1, 1916, she walked to her plant with a light heart. There, she was astounded to see archaic presses with which to print a paper for a circulation of only about 600 customers. The *Democrat* was the smallest of the three Greeneville weeklies, and the larger of her two competitors wrote, "*The Greeneville Democrat* is now being managed by a woman. It will not be alive when the roses bloom again."[3]

At age twenty-six, she had entered into a male-dominated business world where female heads of companies were virtually non-existent. Both of her competitors were Republican businessmen, in a heavily Republican county. Even the name of her paper was an obstacle.

But Edith Susong was a very determined woman. Although she lacked newspaper experience, she was very intelligent and congenial, had a strong and sustaining Christian faith, and had developed writing skills from her mother's tutelage and her school days in Richmond and at Agnes Scott. In addition, she was a natural saleswoman, with a positive and industrious spirit.[4] She assumed the duties of reporting and writing the news, selling subscriptions, and designing and selling advertising. She also kept the books, did the collecting, and often ran the press.

She worked hard, and the community responded to her. By May 1920, she was able to buy one of her competitors. But she lacked the funds to buy the largest local weekly, *The Greeneville Sun*, when it became available later that year.

To solve the problem, her parents agreed to join her. Together, they bought the *Sun* and merged the three weeklies into a daily she named *The Greeneville Democrat-Sun*. Her mother, Quincy Marshall O'Keefe, became the newspaper's main editorial voice; her father, William H. O'Keefe, a former banker, reluctantly became business manager; and Edith herself served as publisher.[5] The name of the paper was changed on December 8, 1930, to *The Greeneville Sun*, with no political affiliation.

The marriage itself did not survive. Edith and Dave were divorced in 1923, after a few years of separation during which she and the children had lived with her parents.

Edith continuously published the newspaper until she died on June 17, 1974, at eighty-four. Her son-in-law, John M. Jones, who had long since become her co-owner and business partner, and who succeeded her as publisher after her death, had assisted her since late 1945.[6] Her father had died in 1937 and her mother in 1958. The circulation of the *Sun*, and the staff, grew substantially over the decades, but she continued to be deeply involved in both business decision making and news reporting.

In addition, for some twenty-five years she wrote an extremely popular, unsigned weekly column that she called "Cheerful Chatter." She completed what proved to be her last column on the Friday morning before, unexpectedly, she died the following Monday. Over that weekend, from a hospital bed, she also conferred with her son-in-law about the purchase of a new press for the *Sun*.

Susong was supportive of women's clubs, having joined Greeneville's Cherokee Club, the leading local women's civic organization, at the age of nineteen. She helped found the Andrew Johnson Women's Club, a federated club, and served as president of the Tennessee Federation of Women's Clubs from 1927–1929. During this period, she was also editor of *The Tennessee Clubwoman*, the forerunner of the *Tennessee Federation News*. She also used her leadership skills in numerous other organizations both in her community and at the state level.

Meanwhile, in her professional life, she served as a president of the Tennessee Woman's Press and Authors Club and was the person elected to represent Tennessee on the first board of directors of the Southern Newspaper Publishers Association, in the early 1920s.

For more than fifty years, she championed causes in her community in which she believed. One of the first such projects in which she played a significant role was the effort to persuade the Pet Milk Company to locate a plant in Greene County. The effort was successful. In recognition of her leadership, she was asked to help pour the first ceremonial can of milk when the Pet Milk plant officially opened March 15, 1928. It was the county's first industry other than tobacco, and it provided many local jobs, as well as much-needed income for local farm families.

Her energy and effectiveness as a newspaperwoman and in public service brought her honors including the Outstanding Woman Journalist in the US in 1948 by the Women's National Press Club. She was selected as the Outstanding Newspaperwoman of the Nation in 1950.

After her death, she was inducted into the Tennessee Newspaper Hall of Fame, which is co-sponsored by the Tennessee Press Association and the University of Tennessee. Separately, her mother, Quincy Marshall O'Keefe, has also been inducted. The two are the only mother and daughter to have been honored in this way.

Her closing words in her written reflection on the fiftieth anniversary of the beginning of her newspaper career were these: "Today I am looking back over fifty years, years of memories of hard days and happy ones, days of discouragement and satisfaction, days of struggle and inspiration. As I review them, I am overwhelmed with nostalgia on this first day of October, nineteen hundred and sixty-six. With eager anticipation I shall begin tomorrow on fifty more."[7]

Edith O'Keefe Susong's *The Greeneville Sun* has come a long way from that October day when she opened the door to the small weekly paper that had so little on which to build. Today, her son-in-law continues as *Sun* publisher, and two of her grandsons and other family members serve the newspaper in key positions.

This generation of her family aspires to the same dream that a young Edith Susong had as she tripped down the block with wings on her feet ninety-six years ago to create the best newspaper she possibly could for the people of Greeneville and Greene County.

NOTES

[1] Alex S. Jones, "A Family Chronicle," *Brill's Content*, May 2000, 91.

[2] Ibid.

[3] Gregg K. Jones, "Peace & Profit," *Presstime*, February 2000, 36.

[4] John M. Jones, Jr. and Gregg K. Jones, "Memorials," *Historic Greene County, Tennessee and Its People: 1783–1992*, 1992, 414.

[5] Jones, "Peace & Profit," 36.

[6] "The *Democrat-Searchlight-Sun*," *The Greeneville Sun Centennial Edition*, July 1979, 42.

[7] Edith O'Keefe Susong, "But, 'The Democrat' Survived," *The Greeneville Sun Centennial Edition*, July 1979, 56.

ELIZABETH RONA

1891–1981

Atomic Pioneer

PATRICIA A. HOPE

Oak Ridge Associated Universities

Elizabeth Rona

A pioneer in the fields of nuclear chemistry and physics, Elizabeth Rona's scientific career lasted more than six decades, spanned two continents, and influenced science around the world. By the time she arrived in Oak Ridge, Tennessee, in 1950, she had spent a large portion of her life in laboratories working alongside some of the greatest minds of the twentieth century.

Until 1941, Dr. Rona, a Hungarian, lived in Europe where she used her measurement of radioactivity in ocean sediments to determine their geological age. She also worked on the chemistry of a newly discovered element, named polonium. Her work included the making of polonium sources that were used to "smash" atoms in pre-accelerator days. She was on the front lines of isotope discovery and the discovery of fission.[1]

When World War II threatened her homeland in 1941, she managed to obtain a visitor's visa to the United States[2] and became an associate professor at Trinity College (Hartford, Connecticut) where she remained until 1946. At the same time, she held an appointment with the Geophysical Laboratory in Washington DC, where she continued her work on geological dating of ocean sediments. However, a telegram from Brian O'Bryen, professor at the University of Rochester's (New York) Institute of Optics, brought her back to her earlier work of polonium chemistry and source design. The telegram was classified "restricted" and began, "In connection with a certain war work, immediate need has risen for large quantities of polonium. . . ."[3]

Dr. Rona was the world's leading expert on polonium, a peculiar metal — as soft as cream cheese, dangerous to inhale, and difficult to produce.[4] Until then it had been produced only in small laboratory quantities.

Now the war effort wanted "large quantities" for what she would later know as The Manhattan Project. By 1945 this project had nearly forty laboratories and factories across the country and was carried out in extreme secrecy even though the project employed approximately two hundred thousand people.[5] These employees included many known scientists of the day: Albert Einstein, Enrico Fermi, Richard Feynman, J. Robert Oppenheimer, Harold C. Urey, and Elizabeth Rona.

Her first memory of hearing about the atom bomb, Dr. Rona recalled, was while having lunch with a group of nuclear scientists at the University of Rochester. Everyone she was with had worked on some part of the project, not knowing what their results were contributing to. She called it the "best kept secret in history." She said in her book, *How It Came About: Radioactivity, Nuclear Physics, Atomic Energy*, "To keep the atom bomb a secret was almost more of an accomplishment than to make the bomb."[6]

After the war, Dr. Rona worked at Argonne National Laboratory near Chicago and in 1950 joined the special training division of the Oak Ridge Institute of Nuclear Studies (ORINS), now called Oak Ridge Associated Universities (ORAU). Her mission was to educate the ever-growing pool of professionals who needed training in the safe use of radioactive isotopes. The courses were opened to worldwide students in 1954, through President Eisenhower's "Atoms for Peace Program."[7]

Dr. Rona's students may have come from all over the world but if "they didn't listen during her lectures, she would stop and call them out," says her close friend and coworker Dr. John Noakes. "She let them know she expected them to either listen or leave. She gained a lot of respect." Even though she was elderly and somewhat frail when Dr. Noakes worked with her, he said she never "shuffled" but would "walk down the hall as if she were leading an army."[8]

Another colleague and friend Roger Cloutier, a senior scientist and head of professional training at ORAU during Dr. Rona's years in Tennessee, remembers her as "a small, slight woman" but a driving force. "Unlike Ernest Rutherford, the scientist who discovered the atom's small but dense nucleus, and was like a bull in a china shop when in his laboratory," he said, "Elizabeth Rona was meticulous and delicate with her equipment." Cloutier says her book, *How It Came About,* describes some of the great scientific discoveries and breakthroughs of her time.[9]

Dr. Rona's broad-based nuclear knowledge came from working with fellow scientists such as Nobel Prize winners Marie Curie, the discoverer of radium and polonium, and Otto Hahn, who is regarded as "the father of nuclear chemistry."[10]

Dr. Genevieve Roessler, a long-time admirer of Mme. Curie, remembers meeting Elizabeth Rona in Oak Ridge. "I was very nervous," Dr. Roessler recalls. "However, Dr. Rona was so nice, so humble. She served tea and crumpets in her home. I thought she was so important but she treated me like I was the important one. She told me that Mme. Curie was quiet, very professional, and very modest. She made Marie Curie real to me. Here was this woman who had worked with someone like that yet she was so humble about it."[11]

To become a scientist, Dr. Rona had to fight an uphill battle. Most of her peers were men. Her own father Samuel Rona, a physician in Hungary, did not want Elizabeth to become a medical doctor, which was her first desire. "He thought it would be too hard for women." Dr. Rona wrote in her book that she honored his wishes even though her father passed away during her sophomore year at the University of Budapest. Instead of medicine, she chose a career of chemistry and physics, obtaining her PhD at age twenty-one.[12]

During this phase of her career, she was very aware of what she called "limited knowledge and experience." Thus, she made her way to Germany's Technical University of Karlsruhe where she worked with other postgraduate students. She said that she intended to study under the top chemist of the day, George Bredig, although fellow students urged her to consider studying instead with Kasimir Fajans. "After all," they told her, "his work (radioactivity) is new and exciting."[13]

Dr. Rona wrote that Fajans "inspired students in a way that made their work more adventurous," while Bredig was more the "authoritative German Professor" type. When Bredig invited students to his home where his wife served tasty German cakes, Dr. Rona was the only scientific woman yet she would have to join the women after dinner to talk about "children, cooking preserves, and exchanging recipes." What she really wanted to do was join her colleagues to "hear and talk shop."[14]

On the other hand, Dr. Rona said Fajans "gave many small parties in the laboratory with no discrimination against women."[15]

Widely published in scientific journals, in 1979, Dr. Rona wrote an article for the *Health Physics Journal*, titled "Laboratory Contamination in the Early Period of Radiation Research." This article sheds light on how the lack of proper instruments for environmental monitoring and a lack of understanding of exposure levels allowed complacency and absence of concern for workers' health in many of the laboratories where she worked, including those in the United States in the 1940s. Dr. Rona's sharing of what she saw and experienced helped bring about a stricter set of radiation safety standards.[16]

She worked in such chemical labs as the Kaiser Wilhelm Institute near Berlin (1922), which had "countless little drops of mercury in the cracks of the old wooden flooring" and the Radium Institute of Vienna (1926), "where the walls and floor of the laboratory were contaminated with Pb-210, Bi-210, and Po-210 (highly radiotoxic forms of lead, bismuth, and polonium)."[17]

While at the Kaiser Institute, Dr. Rona expressed her fears to Director Stefan Meyer that tubes containing radium salts had been improperly packaged and asked for gas masks to help protect her and a coworker. Meyer laughed at her concerns and assured her the tubes were safe. She bought two masks with her own money, which saved her and Dr. Gustav Ortner from severe chemical burns when both tubes exploded, contaminating the room beyond recovery.[18]

The Curie Institute, where Dr. Rona worked in 1929, did not have the safest conditions either, and Dr. Rona describes Mme. Curie as "sitting day after day meticulously weighing radiochloride salts for secondary standards." Despite prolonged exposure, Mme. Curie lived to be sixty-seven, although her fingers were severely burned and periodically she had spells of fatigue and weakness.[19]

After leaving ORAU in 1965, Dr. Rona worked another ten years for the University of Miami, performing the science of radiogeo-chronology she had started in 1928 with Swedish oceanographer Hans Pettersson.[20] She came back to Oak Ridge when she retired the second time and began work on her long-awaited book. *How It Came About* contains no references.

In a memorial, her colleague Marshall Brucer, MD, who had headed the ORINS Medical Division, mentioned that her book really needed no references or footnotes, "for most of the great events happened when either she or one of her close personal friends was there."[21]

In her biography Dr. Rona reflects on the great scientists she worked with. "The most outstanding trait that all great scientists I have known had in common is imagination: all of them were able to see things which would not be obvious but which one had to perceive in a visionary way."[22]

Her long and productive life ended in an Oak Ridge nursing home on July 27, 1981; Elizabeth Rona was ninety-one.[23]

NOTES

[1] Dr. Marshall Brucer, first Director of Medical Division, ORAU, "In Memoriam, Elizabeth Rona (1891?–1981)," *The Journal of Nuclear Medicine*, 23, no. 1, 78.

[2] Dr. Elizabeth Rona, *How It Came About: Radioactivity, Nuclear Physics, Atomic Energy* (Oak Ridge Associated Universities, June 1978), 53.

[3] Ibid., 56.

[4] Ruth H. Howes and Caroline L. Herzenberg, *Their Day in the Sun, Women of The Manhattan Project* (Temple University, 2003), 89.

[5] The Manhattan Project website: http://gk12.rice.edu/trs/science/Atom/man.htm.

[6] Rona, 54–55.

[7] William G. Pollard, Executive Director, 1947–1974, Oak Ridge Associated Universities, Foreword, *How It Came About: Radioactivity, Nuclear Physics, Atomic Energy.*

[8] John Noakes, PhD, Director, Center for Applied Isotope Studies, The University of Georgia, personal interview, July 2, 2012.

[9] Roger Cloutier, former Senior Scientist and Head of Professional Training, ORAU, personal interview, June 27, 2012.

[10] About.com History of Chemistry, http://chemistry.about.com/od/historyofchemistry/a/Who-Is-The-Father-Of-Chemistry.htm.

[11] Dr. Genevieve Roessler, Professor Emeritus, Nuclear Engineering Dept., University of Florida and Editor, Ask-the-Experts Feature, Health Physics Society, personal interview, July 3, 2012.

[12] Rona, 2–3.

[13] Rona, 3.

[14] Rona, 4.

[15] Ibid.

[16] Elizabeth Rona, "Laboratory Contamination In the Early Period of Radiation Research," *Health Physics*, 37, (Pergamon Press Ltd., December 1979).

[17] Ibid., 724.

[18] Ibid., 725.

[19] Ibid.

[20] Rona, *How It Came About: Radioactivity*, 59.

[21] Brucer, 79.

[22] Rona, 49.

[23] Obituary, Elizabeth Rona, *The Oak Ridger* (July 29, 1981).

Susan B. Riley

1896–1973

Let Us Be Up and Doing

Margaret B. Emmett

AAUW Archives

Susan B. Riley

L egendary Susan B. Riley serves as a reminder of George Peabody College's super teachers.[1] She was a trailblazer as the first woman to head a department (English) other than home economics or nursing at Peabody and the first woman dean of the graduate school. She also has the distinction of being the first and only Tennessee woman elected national president of the American Association of University Women (AAUW).[2]

Susan Riley was born in Brookhaven, Mississippi, on May 1, 1896—daughter of Baptist minister George W. Riley and Lily Waller Riley, dean of women at a local college. She attended George Peabody College for Teachers in Nashville and received BS, MA,[3] and PhD[4] degrees in English. She followed the example of her parents, both teachers and administrators in Mississippi colleges, by joining the Peabody faculty in 1928.[5] At Peabody, she rose to chair the English Department in 1948 and became dean of Peabody's graduate school in 1964.

Riley's students at Peabody appreciated her classroom skills. "She made the words on the page come alive," said one former student.[6] She was described as "regal, a demanding mentor, a fascinating lecturer, and a fair and compassionate instructor."[7] Her sense of humor was evident in her lectures. In a 2001 survey, a number of her former students chose her as their favorite professor and wrote of her influence on them. One alumna spoke of Riley's "exterior and interior beauty,"[8] saying that her exterior beauty was exhibited in her dress, carriage, and speech while her interior beauty was shown in her intelligence, knowledge of literature, and the kindness and personal interest she showed to her students. In 2006, a Peabody College alumna set up an endowment in Riley's name at Peabody. Riley encouraged students with her mantra "let us be up and doing" because her classes had so much material to cover in a term.[9] She never wasted time in the courses she taught. An instructor who made a lasting impression on her students, Riley produced exceptional teachers.

Riley was dedicated to the South. In 1935, she organized a workers conference sponsored by AAUW of Tennessee in Cookeville on "Economic Problems of the South" and prepared an outline for a study, "The South."[10] From 1943–1945 she served as president of the Tennessee Folklore Society. During her term of office she gave an address titled "The Teacher and the Folk Arts," a powerful statement of the dignity of all cultures that remains useful today. Riley promoted the South and its geography and culture through books. In an article for teachers, she wrote, "One must be informed through its literature of the South's history and geography, the possibilities and limitations implicit in its economy, and above all its varied social groups and strata." She prepared bibliographies emphasizing the land and the names of those identified with the history and accomplishments of the region.[11] Although Riley was devoted to the South and the aspirations of all its peoples, she often lent her articulate voice, pen, and calming personality to help Peabody College reach out to all.[12]

Riley became one of the national leaders of AAUW, a potent organization for women academics. During the mid-1940s when women's organizations were struggling with admitting African American women to membership, Riley feared that precipitous AAUW board action toward integration would result in crippling of the national program for the improvement of educational opportunities for all women. She observed that the adoption of a new idea is determined as much by emotional receptivity as it is by intellectual truth. In December 1946, the national AAUW board ruled to base eligibility for membership solely on educational criteria. Local branches of AAUW could no longer discriminate in membership policies. The board set a May 1948 deadline for implementing this policy.[13] Within

AAUW, Riley outlined objectives that included obtaining accreditation of more colleges within the southern area and mobilizing for the improvement of public education in those states.[14]

Dr. Riley was the second Southern woman to head the national AAUW organization. Her election proved unusual, as she was the first national president with a degree from a teacher's college. While president, Riley pushed AAUW to "stand apart from the tendency to conformity and consensus."[15] She demonstrated a commitment to nonconformity throughout her professional life and AAUW career. In the October 1952 *AAUW Journal*, she wrote, "the world has the right to expect of institutions and organizations such as ours, moral courage, intellectual clarity . . . and a candid and intrepid thinking about fundamental issues."[16]

During Riley's presidency at AAUW, she presided over the formation of the irrevocable trust known as the Fellowships Endowment Fund of the American Association of University Women. It was to ensure in perpetuity the use of the proceeds in advancing the education of women.[17] This fund is now among the world's largest sources of funding for graduate women.[18]

Riley was very concerned about attacks on the loyalty of teachers during the height of the McCarthy years. She urged AAUW to defend public education and schoolteachers. In 1953, under her leadership, the *AAUW Journal* published a statement entitled "The Communist Threat to Freedom and Democracy."[19]

Riley was president of AAUW when the Supreme Court ordered schools to integrate. She encouraged AAUW branches to act as mediators in their communities. In fact, her Nashville branch carefully planned every step of the process of integration and was the most successful branch in the nation at integrating itself. Their plan became the model for other branches. Riley believed initially that the question of desegregation could be better handled at the local than the national level. However, as time went on and reactions became increasingly bitter, she came to believe that the federal government and national organizations such as AAUW should play stronger roles. She wrote to a fellow board member, "If we had any sort of national leadership—and I don't mean AAUW—in the past two years we needn't have been in quite the mess we are in now." She was critical of President Eisenhower's handling of the school crisis. She suggested that the president get "off the great white father pedestal" and exert some leadership, albeit unpopular.[20]

She served a four-year term at the helm of AAUW during which she was recognized for her intellect, charm, and diligence in carrying out the duties of the presidency. She lived up to her mantra "let us be up and doing." In 1958, the SouthEast Region established an AAUW endowment fund named for her.[21] From 1955 to 1957, she was the only woman to serve on the Congressional Committee on Government Security. First Lady Jacqueline Kennedy invited Riley to be one of her advisers in 1960. She later served from 1963–1965 as the chairman of the committee for fellowships to American women.[22]

After a long and distinguished career, Dr. Riley retired from Peabody in August 1965 and returned to her beloved state of Mississippi where she died December 20, 1973, at the age of seventy-seven. She was buried in Clinton Cemetery in Clinton, Hinds County, Mississippi in the same cemetery as her parents and her sister Mary Belle Riley King.[23]

NOTES

[1] Teacher's colleges were women's colleges that trained teachers. These colleges were not considered academically comparable to other types of colleges/universities. Many women attended these colleges because teaching was one of the few careers open to women.

[2] The American Association of University Women was founded in 1881 for college women graduates. Today it has 150,000 members who promote equity for women and girls. American Association of University Women Online Museum. https://svc.aauw.org/museum/, accessed October 2012.

[3] Susan B. Riley, "A Critical Study of Amy Lowell's Experiments in Verse Forms," Thesis (MA), Department of English, Graduate School of Education, George Peabody College for Teachers, August, 1928.

[4] Susan B. Riley, "The Life and Works of Albert Pike to 1860," Vols. 1–3, bibliography at end of Vol. 2. Thesis (PhD) George Peabody College for Teachers, 1934.

[5] "Obituaries," *The Nashville Banner*, December 20, 1973.

[6] "The Susan B. Riley Scholarship," *Peabody Reflector*, Vanderbilt Peabody College, Donor Report, Fall 2009, http://www.vanderbilt.edu/magazines/peabody-reflector/2009/11/donors/, accessed October 2012.

[7] Ibid.

[8] "Your Favorite Professors," *The Peabody Reflector*, Spring 2001, 20, www.vanderbilt.edu/magazines/peabody-reflector/2001-spring-reflector.

[9] "The Susan B. Riley Scholarship," *The Peabody Reflector*, Donor Report Fall, 2009. www.vanderbilt.edu/magazines/peabody-reflector/2009/11/donors.

[10] Susan B. Riley, "The South," a bibliography prepared for the Tennessee branches of the American Association of University Women, 1938.

[11] Susan B. Riley, "Knowing the South through Books," *Peabody Journal of Education,* 18, 1, 1940. http://www.tandfonline.com/doi/abs/10.1080/01619564009535607, accessed October 2012.

[12] Jesse Burt, "Á Preliminary Bibliography of Dr. Susan B. Riley," *The Peabody Reflector,* Spring 1973.

[13] Susan Levine, *Degrees of Equality* (Philadelphia: Temple University Press, 1995), 79–80.

[14] Accreditation was crucial because membership in AAUW was restricted to graduates of colleges that had been approved by the Association of Collegiate Alumni (ACA). Requirements for being approved were that all members of the college's teaching staff had to hold degrees from colleges in good standing and the admission requirements of a college had to include at least four years of serious secondary school work. Emphasis was on a liberal arts education.

[15] Levine, *Degrees,* 79, 80.

[16] Susan B. Riley, *Journal of American Association of University Women,* October 1952.

[17] AAUW online Museum, https://svc.aauw.org/museum/history/1950_1959/index.cfm. accessed October 2012.

[18] In the 2012–2013 academic year, AAUW was providing more than $4.3 million in funding for more than 278 fellowships and grants to outstanding women and nonprofit organizations. http://www.aauw.org/learn/fellows_directory/, accessed October 2012.

[19] "AAUW Historic Principles" at www.aauw.org/learn/publications/upload/historicprinciples.pdf, 11.

[20] Levine, *Degrees*, 133.

[21] Nancy Knaus, Southeast Central Region Regional History Project, Knoxville, Tennessee, June 1992.

[22] Margie LeCoultre, "The Tennessee Division of AAUW 1926–1985," Tennessee AAUW, 1985, 28.

[23] Social Security Death Index and www.Find-A-Grave.com.

MARY "MOLLY" HART KIMBALL MASSIE TODD

1904–1998

Face of a Grandmother, Heart of a Saint, Soul of a Warrior

CAROLE STANFORD BUCY

Courtesy of the *Nashville Banner*

Molly Todd

Regarded as a communist to some and a heroine to others, Molly Todd took an active role in political events in Tennessee from the time of her arrival in 1939 until the time of her death in 1998. She worked to bring birth control to Nashville and was an advocate for mental health services, governmental reform, and desegregation. She was a tireless crusader who became a role model for the next generation of women who led the second wave of feminism.

Mary "Molly" Hart Kimball grew up in Utica, New York, in a traditional middle-class family. An excellent student, Molly won a scholarship to all-female Vassar College. In an interview with historian Elisabeth Perry in 1985, Molly Todd recalled that she had planned to become a doctor when she entered Vassar but found the memorization of formulae in her chemistry classes "boring." Her roommate's father, a doctor, discouraged her from pursuing a career in medicine, telling her, "Women in medicine are a survival of the unfit!" She never forgot this negative comment as a painful example of society's views of the limits of a woman's ability.[1]

In early 1927, while visiting a Vassar friend in Lexington, Kentucky, she met her two future husbands, Robert Massie and James Todd. The following year, Molly moved to Kentucky and married Robert Massie, director of the Massie School in Versailles, Kentucky. Within two years of the wedding, Robert Massie died of cancer at the age of thirty-nine. At the time of Massie's death, the couple had one fifteen-month-old son, Robert Massie, III. A week later, Molly gave birth to a second son, Kimball Massie. Molly later renewed her friendship with James Todd, the best man at her wedding to Robert Massie, and in 1936, they married.

It was in Lexington that Molly first encountered racism and the second-class status of African Americans. Accepted by whites without question, she found the practice of racial separation quite puzzling. Using the experience she gained working on the board of a maternal health clinic in New Jersey, she became involved in a campaign in Lexington to open a birth control clinic. When the clinic opened at Good Samaritan Hospital, it offered services for black and white women alike, but the races did not come on the same day of the week. She regularly visited local doctors who provided care for pregnant women and delivered babies to solicit these doctors' support for the clinic. Her Lexington friends who had grown up and lived their entire lives in the South were shocked to find out that Molly had gone alone to call on Bush Hunter, a black physician in the city. White Southern women simply did not do this. In this act, Molly Todd had crossed the invisible line, the impenetrable barrier of race that divided the South.

In 1939, the Todds moved to Nashville. Her husband was a manager with Harvey's Department Store so she was eligible to participate in elite social activities. Ora Mann, an organizer who worked for the National Birth Control League and was the founder of the Planned Parenthood Federation of Tennessee, had been unable to establish a birth control clinic in Nashville. When Mann met Molly Todd, she quickly realized that Molly would be an asset to her movement. She appointed Molly to be the president of the Tennessee Maternal Health Association.[2] "Birth control was not an accepted idea in the late 1930s," recalled Todd forty years later. "It was no one's business how many babies you had."[3]

Once Planned Parenthood was established in Nashville, Molly Todd moved on to mental health issues. When the state public health commission failed to acknowledge that mental health was a special problem, Molly joined forces with other mental health advocates to lobby the general assembly for a separate department of mental health. A separate department became a reality when Frank Clement became governor. Molly Todd served as a member of both the Nashville and Tennessee Mental Health Association boards, and chaired the steering committee that established the Nashville Mental Health Center (now known as the Dede Wallace Center).

Perhaps it was inevitable that Molly Todd's social activism would lead her to the political arena. As founder and first president of the Nashville League of Women Voters in 1948, she began a lifelong advocacy for more women in politics. In 1952, when Tennessee called its first state constitutional convention since Reconstruction, Molly Todd decided to run as a delegate to the convention. She won; at the 1953 convention, she was one of only four women delegates. When the convention ended, she immediately joined the local campaign in support of the amendments that the convention proposed.

A major political issue in Tennessee in the early 1950s was the subject of redistricting, the process by which the members of the general assembly drew the lines to create legislative districts. Although this process was supposed to happen every ten years after the completion of the United States census, the district boundaries had not been redrawn since 1901. In spite of the rapidly shifting population to cities, the membership of the Tennessee General Assembly remained overwhelmingly rural. Citizens who lived in heavily populated urban areas simply had less representation. Molly Todd joined forces with a group of young lawyers who decided to challenge Tennessee's failure to reapportion the districts in court and became a plaintiff in the landmark Supreme Court decision of *Baker v. Carr*, now known as the "One Man, One Vote" case.[4] In this landmark decision, the high court ruled that state legislatures must apportion equitably their legislative districts so that each district had approximately the same number of voters.

After the Supreme Court's 1954 *Brown v. the Board of Education of Topeka* decision declared school segregation unconstitutional, Nashville had to confront its policies of racism that permeated every aspect of life. Molly Todd had opposed segregation through-out her life; she wholeheartedly joined the local civil rights move-ment. After college students began to participate in sit-ins at local lunch counters in downtown Nashville, Molly Todd joined them. Realizing that other employees criticized her husband, Jim Todd, a senior manager of Harvey's Department Store, for her activities, she wrote a personal letter to Fred Harvey saying that she did not want her husband to suffer for her actions. Harvey, who was from Canada, was not a segregationist even though his stores had segre-gated lunch counters. Harvey responded with a letter of support. With this support, she led the sit-ins at the downtown store. When Harvey's Department Store repainted its restrooms, Jim Todd per-suaded the painters to leave off the signs "colored" and "white." The signs were quietly removed from restrooms and water foun-tains without incident and integration was accomplished.[5]

When Molly Todd died in 1998, *The Tennessean* summed up how many Nashvillians saw Molly Todd, "Molly Todd had the face of a grandmother, the heart of a saint, and the soul of a warrior." The list of her accomplishments reached almost every facet of public life in Nashville. "Molly Todd was fearless," the editors went on to say. "She did whatever she needed to do to make her point—whether it was standing toe-to-toe with the most powerful person in this state or sitting quietly with black students at a lunch counter. Her strength was contagious."[6] Molly Todd was willing to take a public position on matters of injustice and to work for things in which she believed. Her courage and example paved the way for women in Tennessee to enter the political arena at every level. One can imag-ine that nothing would have made Molly happier than to have wit-nessed Barak Obama's election as President. Her work had helped pave the way.

NOTES

[1] Molly Hart Kimball Massie Todd, interview by Elisabeth I. Perry, March 8, March 15, March 22, and June 4, 1985, unpublished summary of interview in possession of the author.

[2] Bill Turner, "Class, Controversy, and Contraceptives: Birth Control Advocacy in Nashville, Tennessee, 1932–1944," *Tennessee Historical Quarterly*, 53 (1994).

[3] Perry interview.

[4] Gene Graham, *One Man One Vote: Baker v. Carr and the American Levellers* (Boston: Little, Brown and Company, 1972).

[5] Perry interview.

[6] "Molly Todd, Advocate," editorial, *The Tennessean*, April 22, 1998.

JUNE SUTTON ANDERSON

1926–1984

A Tireless Advocate for Women

REBECCA CAWOOD MCINTYRE

MTSU Creative and Visual Services

June Sutton Anderson

Educator, scientist, and activist June Sutton Anderson fought tenaciously for women's rights in Tennessee and greatly influenced higher education. As professor at Middle Tennessee State University, she fought for equity and the end of gender discrimination in academia. In 1980, she publically challenged the academic community to work for the equal recognition of women. "We must work to serve as outstanding role models for our women students and work to be 'super women' if that is what it takes to achieve equal recognition in academe," Anderson claimed. "We can rest in retirement and, finally, continue to rock the boat of patriarchy and pack the boat until it is overloaded and calls for a bigger one."[1]

Born in 1926, June Anderson grew up in Lauderdale County in West Tennessee, an only child in a middle-class household. Her parents, George and Leliah Sutton, nurtured her intellectual endeavors and encouraged her to study and seek a career at the time when white Southern society expected women to make marriage and children women's only aspiration. Anderson excelled at school and entered George Peabody College for Teachers in Nashville. In 1947, she earned a BS in chemistry and biology, and the following year Peabody awarded her an MS in chemistry and English. In 1954, she earned a second undergraduate degree in physics. Anderson began her teaching career at Howard High School in south Nashville. She spent the next ten years at the school winning numerous teaching awards, honors that attest to her level of commitment and expertise. In 1954, she won a coveted General Electric Fellowship for Physics. In 1957, she won the Tennessee Distinguished Science Teacher Award and a year later received a grant to study physics from the National Science Foundation.

The year she received her grant, Anderson made an important career decision. She left secondary education and became an assistant professor at Middle Tennessee State College (now Middle

Tennessee State University) where she taught chemistry and physics in the science department. Women professors in higher education were rare, particularly in the male-dominated field of science. Anderson had the distinction of being the first woman in the science department, and she remained the only female chemistry professor for over two decades. She stayed at MTSU for the rest of her career, leaving only briefly to study at Florida State University where she earned a PhD in chemistry and statistics in 1964.

As a scientist, Anderson specialized in inorganic chemistry. She began research in x-ray powder diffraction of inorganic materials, an analytical technique used to identify crystalline matter. She rose to the rank of full professor in the 1970s. Although an excellent researcher, Anderson was foremost an educator and focused most of her energy on her students. She especially encouraged women to join the science program. One of her former graduate students, Valerie R. Avent, realized that Anderson was not only accomplished but also tenacious. "She was driven, and 'No' was not an option," Avent recalled.[2] An MTSU colleague, Ayne Cantrell remembers that June was "like a pit bull. When she sunk her teeth into something she wouldn't let go until she got some satisfaction."[3]

In the late 1970s, without abandoning her students, Anderson shifted her focus to activism. Her first goal was to help women professionals. She organized and became the first president of the Concerned Faculty and Administrative Women, a group created to aid post-secondary women educators and staff on campus. CFAW's main goals addressed inequities in pay and promotions for female faculty. At MTSU, as at many universities, women were paid less than men and remained at the lowest ranks longer than their male counterparts.

In 1975, Anderson and CFAW conducted an official survey of pay rates at MTSU for male and female faculty members. The salary study revealed that of the 432 full-time faculty members, only ninety-two were women and only ten of these women held the highest rank of professor. Most women were concentrated in a few departments, with only home economics having a majority of female faculty members. Of the twenty-six departments housed at MTSU, six departments—aerospace, criminal justice, geography, industrial arts, mass communications, and philosophy—had no women faculty at all.[4] The study also revealed that the school paid women at least $500 less than their male counterparts, and often the disparity was in the thousands. This study gained the attention of the federal government. Anderson testified before the National Advisory Council on Women's Educational Programs, a group appointed by the president to evaluate discriminatory policies in education. As a result of CFAW's commitment to equity in pay, the Equal Employment Opportunity Commission awarded thirty-five faculty women with compensatory back pay and adjusted salaries.[5] Beyond the MTSU campus, in 1980 Anderson helped form a statewide group for women educators. This group, Women in Higher Education in Tennessee, supports professional development through networking.[6]

Besides working on behalf of professional women, Anderson also strove for equal opportunities for female students, particularly mature women trying to transition back into higher education or to begin college for the first time. To aid these women, she founded the Women Information Service for Education in 1977, an immediately successful advocacy center for women. WISE began modestly in a small room on campus with a volunteer staff composed mainly of members of CFAW. The WISE Center offered support and encouragement for women through workshops, counseling, job referrals, and legal clinics. Students were helped in a variety of ways, including how to write a resume and where to seek legal help. Other WISE projects included a daycare that Anderson founded along with Dr. Jan Hayes and Dr. Janet Camp in 1981. Anderson won a $250,000 grant in 1979 so that WISE could offer more services, including a basic skills workshop for women with a tenth grade education or above. In 1978 Anderson was also a founding professor and first coordinator of the women's studies program at MTSU.[7]

Anderson, who spoke so passionately about waiting to rest in retirement, never had a chance to rest herself. Since childhood, she had suffered from asthma. In the early 1980s, she had contracted emphysema. By November 1983, Anderson's doctors told her to stop working completely. That month, Anderson wrote to her colleagues that she needed to resign from her committees and that each resignation "tears a new hole in me." She lapsed into a coma in late December and passed away on January 11, 1984, with her mother by her side.[8]

Anderson left a tremendous legacy to the women of Tennessee. The organizations she created or co-created are still going strong. The CFAW changed its name to the Association for Faculty and Administrative Women. WHET recently merged with the American Council on Education. Every year ACE presents the June Anderson Award that recognizes an individual's contributions in promoting equality for women in higher education. At MTSU, the June Anderson Foundation awards several scholarships for women age twenty-three and older who want to enter traditionally underrepresented fields. WISE was renamed the June Anderson Women's Center in 1984 to honor its founder and visionary leader. Its name was recently updated to the June Anderson Center for Women and Non-Traditional Students to reflect its wider scope. Certainly, Anderson would be pleased to know that her message of women's equity and self-fulfillment is still alive in Tennessee and that her efforts at gender equality have succeeded beyond even her ambitious dreams.[9,10]

NOTES

[1] Angie Galloway, "CFAW Working for the Equality of All Women," *Sidelines* 54, no. 5 (September 5, 1980): 1.

[2] Valerie Avent, interviewed by Rebecca Cawood McIntyre, Murfreesboro, TN, May 10, 2012.

[3] Clara Rasmussen, "June Anderson: Women's Rights Pioneer," *Sidelines* 86, no. 14 (October 21, 2009): 5.

[4] John Pitts, "Washington Probes MTSU Job Bias," *Sidelines* 50, no. 3 (June 22, 1976): 1.

[5] Mopsy Gascon and Bill Fisher, "All That She Left Behind," *MTSU Magazine* (Fall/Winter 2002): 5.

[6] Rasmussen, 5.

[7] Gascon and Fisher, 5.

[8] Rasmussen, 5.

[9] Middle Tennessee State University, Midlander 1998 Yearbook (Murfreesboro, TN: Graduating Class of 1998), 2.

[10] Rebecca Cawood McIntyre and Nancy Rupprecht, "Learn to Stand Alone: Women on Campus," in *Middle Tennessee State University, A Centennial Legacy*, edited by Janice Leone (Nashville: Twin Oaks Press, 2011), 53–86.

Margaret "Peggy" Thompson Heddleson

1928–2009

Let the Inside Voice Speak

Ann Thornfield-Long

Courtesy of Fred Heddleson Family

Peggy Heddleson

Margaret "Peggy" Thompson Heddleson achieved acclaim as an artist in ceramics, painting, and basket weaving, but she found her greatest fulfillment in making cloth banners with words. The emotions shown in these banners brought people, especially women, new ways to think about themselves and ways to heal. In 1968, she co-founded the Foothills Craft Guild, the oldest fine art craft guild in Tennessee. The guild continues to provide an important regional venue for juried artists to promote and market their work.[1]

Peggy herself was an abused wife, a cancer survivor, an adoptive parent, and later a single mother. Peggy was an advocate for women and children, investing her time and resources with organizations that helped women, especially women's shelters. She also volunteered at the Oak Ridge Children's Museum, designing a life-sized playhouse and special places where children could explore their own feelings and artistic abilities.

As a girl of Norwegian descent growing up in Minnesota, she and her twin brother were very active. In a childhood accident, Peggy's permanent front teeth were knocked out by a wooden swing.[2] When other girls were smiling for pictures, Peggy could not smile or speak without embarrassment until her teeth were replaced with false ones.

In high school, she suffered a second blow to her self-image. She faced the fear of an early death when a large tumor was discovered in her abdomen. Surgery saved her life but left her unable to have children. This was during the 1940s when, instead of looking forward to a career, most young women were expected to find fulfillment in becoming wives and mothers. Peggy struggled to feel lovable. She wondered if anyone would want to marry someone who couldn't have children.[3]

After high school, Peggy studied art at St. Olaf College, a Lutheran college not far from her home. There she met and fell in love with a young man who was studying science. Peggy was reluctant to tell him she could not have children, but he reassured her that it didn't matter to him. He told her they could adopt children. The two married, but before they were married a year, he was drafted to fight in the Korean War.

When Peggy's husband came home from the war, they adopted two sons and a daughter. Peggy wrote:

> **Real Mother**
> *They tell me*
> *how to hold babies*
> *the "real" way*
> *to hold them*
> *because I'm not*
> *a "real" mother*
> *I haven't given birth*
> *years of crying*
> *didn't count....*[4]

Peggy had looked forward to this family of her dreams, but her husband came home from the war a changed and scarred man. He criticized her for what seemed like everything, even the way she loaded the dishwasher. Those things hurt, but when he criticized her for not being able to have children, her heart was pierced. Still she stayed with him. Her diary records nineteen moves across the country with the children and their pets crowded into the back seat of the car. Their last move brought them to Oak Ridge, Tennessee.[5]

When he threatened to hurt a pet, she became frightened. His words escalated to physical abusiveness, but Peggy stuck it out. Finally, she saw what the abuse was doing to her children, and she knew she had to leave. Peggy wrote about the trauma of her escape in her diary. She loaded her car with children and sleeping bags and fled to a safe place.[6]

Now a single mother of three, Peggy sold her art at shows, taking the children along. They would cheer when she sold something. Like other divorced families, they got by. In her spare moments, Peggy wrote snippets in her diary. Those snippets of words and thoughts later became the inspiration for the short sayings on her banners. She talked about her marriage being a "continual clenched fist," and said that she and her husband "smoldered like a compost pile," noting "I have enough fertilizer to write about for the rest of my life." She got counseling and wrote, "What a relief to have someone to listen. I decided to just lay back and enjoy it."[7]

It was at a church women's conference that Peggy first thought about banners. She could not sit still long enough to attend the conference, but wanting to help, she washed the dishes. One woman came to the kitchen and told her she might like a banner that was hanging upstairs. Peggy went to see it and though she found the banner itself unattractive, she loved the flow of words. Now she wondered, "Could banners be art?" She wrote:

> *I make art*
> *to understand the madness*
> *to let the inside voice speak*
> *to play with my black and white rainbow*
> *to develop my own dictionary*
> *to relieve the pressures of imagination and the curse of courage*
> *to be alone*
> *to sew together friends*
> *I make art because I can.*[8]

Peggy tried to make a banner from burlap — a dismal failure. She experimented with corduroy, cotton, and finally found that felt, especially if it contained wool, worked very well. She adapted the Norwegian woodcraft of rosemaling (painting designs on wood) to fabric. Soon Peggy became an expert on fonts, carefully cutting curling letters from fabric, and sometimes using quilting stitches on a plain background to spell out words that a viewer would not see until they had stared at the banner for a while.

In fits and starts, Peggy created works of art by sewing her fistfuls of words on colorful cloth and thereby found her calling to help other women in distress. Because Peggy had experienced infertility, abuse, adoptive motherhood, and problems with self-esteem, she was able to identify with suffering peculiar to women. Her banners expressed that, and soon women flocked to see them.

In one banner, the words of a book title, *Pain is When it Hurts*, spill onto a pale blue felt that is shredded into strips at the bottom. When Peggy talked and wrote about the banner, she said:

> The emotional pain I went through surviving a broken marriage cannot be described. I was alone in a place far from my parents and childhood friends — I couldn't go sit with a cousin or high school friend on lonely Sunday afternoons. Three half-grown children needed me — and I was too broken to do more than get [through] the day and night. Each day and night I was in a foreign country called Hell, trying to understand a language/experience/emotion whose language I did not speak. Time, Parents Without Partners, thinking and watching helped, and this book title told me it was all right to be this way for a while.[9]

129

On a large burgundy banner, poppies are outlined in yellow. Small white letters on one petal state: "a woman was raped here 1983." Peggy said in the 1960s and 1970s groups of feminists stenciled rape circles on sidewalks where rapes had taken place, noting the date. She first saw one in Minneapolis. She used poppies because war veterans had traditionally made and sold them to earn money for disabled vets. "Men went to war and came back dead, wounded, and insane, with hunks of their lives missing." Peggy believed rape was a war zone for women. When she began traveling to show her banners and give talks about them, more than fifty women confessed to her privately that they had been raped. She said, "I ministered to them as best I could, as gently as I could, with words."

On one banner, the words "OHGODOHGOD" are repeated in a muted pink and burgundy. Over the background in stark white modern script are the words "I am well acquainted with every hour of the night." Peggy's worries often kept her awake until she put them away or they wore themselves out. She said that OH GOD can be both a curse and a prayer.

In a quote she took from James Joyce's *Ulysses*, black letters spill down a gold and white river stating, "Yes I said Yes I will Yes." Peggy had reason to think about those words after meeting Fred Heddleson, a renowned artist in his own right. They had met at a Parents Without Partners meeting, and Fred found many things to love about Peggy, including her straightforward manner. He asked Peggy to marry him, and she said yes to a new life when they married in 1977. Fred scheduled work on his commissioned art projects so that he could often accompany Peggy as she traveled giving her "banner talks" advocating for battered women to church and civic groups. Fred not only helped display the banners, he also watched the crowd for those who couldn't hold back their emotions when

Peggy spoke. He helped Peggy find them after the talks so that if they wanted, she could talk privately with them.

Peggy died in 2009, but her words live on in her banners that can be seen from Tennessee to Iowa. Her words still encourage women to make peace with the past, to use the gift of each woman's unique voice, and to make life a work of art. Peggy's banners are displayed at the Children's Museum of Oak Ridge and at Grace Lutheran Church, Oak Ridge, where her ashes repose in the memorial garden.

NOTES

[1] Foothills Craft Guild, http://foothillscraftguild.org/about-the-guild/.

[2] D. Ray Smith, "Peggy Heddleson—More Than an Artist," *Historically Speaking, Oak Ridger,* April 29, 2011.

[3] Fred Heddleson, "Peggy's Banners: A compilation of photographs and writings in memory of Peggy Heddleson," Unpublished Manuscript, 2011.

[4] Peggy Heddleson, Collection of journals, diaries, and personal papers, owned by Fred Heddleson.

[5] Ibid.

[6] Ibid.

[7] Ibid.

[8] Ibid.

[9] Ibid.

ANNA BELLE CLEMENT O'BRIEN

1923–2009

First Lady of Tennessee Politics

MARGARET JANE POWERS

State of Tennessee Photographic Services

Anna Belle Clement O'Brien

Anna Belle Clement was born on May 6, 1923, in Scottsville, Kentucky. She was endowed with the usual assets and liabilities, a superior education for her time, and a perennially positive outlook. With these advantages plus her ability to recognize an opportunity and work continuously until it was achieved, she became the best-known woman in Tennessee politics on a state and national level and the matriarch of Tennessee's foremost and most powerful political family. She succeeded fully in what was then considered the exclusive province of men, while never sacrificing her femininity. Instead, she employed what are still considered feminine skills—charm, beauty, compassion, and gracious hostessing—to make contacts and further the relationships upon which successful political careers are built.

"Miss Anna Belle" as she was always called, or "ABO" in the shorthand of her staff in written communications to each other, was a joy to know. Always young, always fun, she enjoyed people and appreciated their unique charms, never judging personal choices. She loved to dance, and was quite good, always elegantly dressed and coiffed with a full maquillage,[1] no matter the occasion. Said to be five nine in height, with stilettos and the bouffant hairstyle of the day she stood well over six feet tall with perfect posture. Like Queen Elizabeth I, and to a lesser extent, the current Queen Elizabeth, Margaret Thatcher, and other female world leaders, it was easy to tell at first glance that Miss Anna Belle was in authority, but never imperious. Despite her dignified appearance, regular working people and the poor always identified with her, and she knew, and could call by name, virtually everyone encountered. With beautiful auburn hair and long slim legs, she looked a lot like a young Lucille Ball.

I first met Miss Anna Belle in the late 1960s when she dropped by one afternoon, completely unannounced, to visit at the home of my aunt and uncle, who published a county newspaper. At that time, they thought of her merely as former Governor Frank Clement's sister. They didn't realize it then, but she was laying the initial groundwork to have her new husband, attorney and former State Senator Charles H. O'Brien of Memphis, named to the Tennessee Court of Appeals. When he wasn't named to the post, he ran a statewide campaign for a seat on the appellate court, with Miss Anna Belle at the helm, and won. Anna Belle knew people in every Tennessee county from her years of work in the governor's office for her brother, from 1953 until 1959 and again from 1963 to 1967, in the position that is now known as deputy governor. Judge O'Brien went on to serve as chief justice of the Tennessee Supreme Court.[2]

The next time I met Miss Anna Belle was in 1974, when she came to my family's small newspaper to announce that she was running for an open seat in the state House of Representatives representing our county. She won with a slogan she herself referred to as "corny" emblazoned on a car-top sign, "Of our District she will tell, if you elect Miss Anna Belle." By 1977, when I was selected by the University of Tennessee National Alumni Association to serve as a legislative aide from the UT Graduate School of Political Science to the Ninetieth General Assembly, Miss Anna Belle was a state senator. While she was not the first female member of the Tennessee Senate, she was the first female senate committee chair, first chairing education, then transportation, and the Democratic caucus.[3] Miss Anna Belle's staff routinely served homemade (by various Democratic women's groups) "treats" from an elegant tray to education committee members during each meeting she chaired to insure full and good natured attendance. It worked. Those feminine charms remained ever ready and completely effective during her twenty-two years as a member of the Tennessee General Assembly.

While at the legislature, I became friends with Sara Perry, Miss Anna Belle's niece and a member of her staff. Sara, who subsequently married Memphis State Senator Jim Kyle, won statewide election to become one of Tennessee's three public service commissioners—now called the Tennessee Regulatory Authority.[4] As a friend of Sara's, I became friends with Miss Anna Belle as well. I campaigned with and for Miss Anna Belle (and she campaigned for me), Justice O'Brien married my husband and me, and I drove, flew, or rode with Miss Anna Belle to political events throughout Tennessee. After I graduated from law school in 1980, Miss Anna Belle advised me that her hometown of Crossville in Cumberland County would be the perfect place for a young woman to open a law office, and she was right.

In addition to the usual political events and fundraisers, Miss Anna Belle regularly hosted large brunches and dinner parties at her lakeside home near Crossville, named "O'Brien Harbor." The sprawling house curves around the lakeshore, having grown from a small cabin she had purchased years before as a weekend getaway from her work in Nashville. Those invitations were a mechanism to connect with new people within the region and cement existing relationships. Politics were not on the menu on those dates, with Republicans and Independents in attendance along with us Yellow Dogs,[5] although public events and current issues were always discussed. No one attended for the food, which often consisted of previously frozen spaghetti pie, prepared by various Democrat women. It was for the company, the conversation, and the possible opportunity the events offered that one attended. You never knew who might attend, but you knew they would be doing things that were interesting.

Tables were set up throughout the house—in the den, dining room, and sunroom—everyone served themselves from a large buffet counter bordering the tiny kitchen. The walls of her home were covered with the most incredible photographs of the historic events in which she participated. Also discreetly displayed, in a small frame, was the elegant handwritten note Miss Anna Belle received from First Lady Jacqueline Kennedy, thanking her for the hospitality she had extended while the Kennedys campaigned for president in Nashville. With close inspection, it was astonishing what could be seen among her treasures.

Miss Anna Belle ran for governor of Tennessee in 1982. She lost in the Democratic primary to Knoxville Mayor Randy Tyree, and immediately joined his campaign, working tirelessly. Tyree ultimately lost in the general election to Lamar Alexander, but Miss Anna Belle went on to work with Governor Alexander as chair of the senate education committee to make sweeping improvements to Tennessee's education standards.

Miss Anna Belle had no children, but enjoyed mentoring her nephews — Bob Clement, who preceded his cousin Sara Kyle as a public service commissioner, went on to serve as a member of the TVA board of directors, and later as a Tennessee congressman for several terms, and Frank Clement, Jr., who serves on the Tennessee Court of Appeals. She also helped countless candidates become office holders throughout Tennessee with her advice, leadership, and support. Congressmen Lincoln Davis, Jim Cooper, and John Tanner, as well as Vice President Al Gore, and countless members of the Tennessee Legislature, benefited from her advice.

Disabled children, who at that time received little, if any, public assistance and public education, were Miss Anna Belle's initial areas of primary focus. Governor Clement had been a champion of free schoolbooks for all children in public education. Miss Anna Belle shared his concern that everyone should receive an equal public education. During her first years in Cumberland County, Miss

Anna Belle began to realize that disabled children were not receiving their share of education, and she worked hard before running for office to set up systems to extend their care. While in office, she initiated the concept of mainstreaming the disabled in education.

In the 1980s, Miss Anna Belle was diagnosed with breast cancer and underwent a mastectomy and reconstructive surgery. She used that experience to change the law to require health insurers to provide coverage for mammography and proper breast reconstruction surgery for all Tennessee women.[6]

Politics was a vocation, not an avocation, for Miss Anna Belle, and campaigning continued 24/7, 365 days a year. Even after she retired from her own public career in 1996, her daily schedule of appearances continued to be published, and she attended and participated in everything, just as she always had. She could be seen at Christmas parades in all surrounding counties, campaign events for candidates she supported, Chamber of Commerce legislative breakfasts kicking off each legislative session, annual meeting luncheons of all major organizations, monthly and annual, local and state Democrat women's meetings, the economic summit hosted by the Tennessee Economic Council on Women, presidential and gubernatorial inaugurations, and ribbon cuttings. She completed several public and private events every day of the week. Judge O'Brien sang in the choir at the church he and Miss Anna Belle regularly attended. Countless weddings were performed at their home, with Judge O'Brien officiating at a moment's notice.

Justice O'Brien's death in 2007 affected Miss Anna Belle dramatically. She still kept busy with public appearances in her usual way,[7] and helped anyone who asked for her advice on government issues, but with much more hesitancy. Miss Anna Belle died on August 31, 2009, as the result of a fall at her home. She is buried in Dickson, Tennessee, near the Clement Family History Museum.

NOTES

[1] Makeup; cosmetics (Oxford Dictionary and Thesaurus, American Edition, 1996). From the French: pronounced "mak-ee-ahzh"

[2] "Retired Justice O'Brien dead at 86," *The Commercial Appeal* (Memphis, TN), January 19, 2007.

[3] "2009 Humanitarian Leadership Award Ceremony, honoring Anna Belle Clement O'Brien," Clement Railroad Hotel Museum, www. clementrailroadmuseum.org/award.html.

[4] "Director Sara Kyle," Tennessee Regulatory Authority, www.tn.gov/tra/leadership/kylebio.shtml.

[5] Someone (generally from the South) who would rather vote for a yellow dog than a Republican, www.urbandictionary.com/define.php?term=Yellow Dog Democrat.

[6] "Anna Belle Clement O'Brien, Cumberland County's 'first lady' dies," *Crossville Chronicle* (Crossville, TN), September 23, 2009.

[7] "Anna Belle Clement O'Brien Calls Upon Democrats to Work Harder for Candidates," *Greeneville Sun* (Greeneville, TN), April 1, 2009.

Evelyn Stone Bryan Johnson

1909–2012

Mama Bird

Pam Strickland

Courtesy of Sue Johnson Family

Evelyn Bryan Johnson
Inducted into the National Aviation Hall of Fame

Evelyn "Mama Bird" Bryan Johnson might never have become a world-renowned pilot and flight instructor who spent the equivalent of six and a half years in the air, if not for a restrictive Tennessee law about married teachers during the Depression.

When she died on May 10, 2012, Evelyn was 102 and recognized by the *Guinness Book of World Records* as having flown 57,685.4 hours—more than any other woman alive or dead.[1] The only man who had more hours, Ed Long of Montgomery, Alabama, who had 64,000 hours, had reportedly died saying "Don't let that woman get more flying time than I've got."[2]

Evelyn Elizabeth Stone was born on November 4, 1909, in Corbin, Kentucky, one of three children of Edward William Lockard Stone, a conductor on the Louisville and Nashville Railroad, and Mayme Fox Stone, a public school teacher. The family moved to Etowah, Tennessee, in 1915. Evelyn went to Tennessee Wesleyan College in Athens, Tennessee, on scholarship, earning a degree in English in 1929. That same year, she saw her first airplane, an American Standard. She took a ride in the open cockpit plane and thought it was a "great adventure." She went on to teach sixth grade in Etowah for two years.[3]

While taking a summer class at the University of Tennessee at Knoxville, she met Wyatt Jennings (W. J.) Bryan. They married on March 21, 1931, and then both studied at the University of Texas in Austin before settling in Jefferson City, Tennessee. Evelyn couldn't immediately return to teaching because state law barred married women from the classroom during the first five years of marriage. So the couple borrowed $250 from W. J.'s father and started College Cleaning, a dry-cleaning business near the Carson Newman College campus.[4]

The eighteen-hour days got longer in 1941 when W. J. joined the US Army after Pearl Harbor, leaving Evelyn to run the business by herself.[5] "It was getting tiresome. Two and a half years," she told an interviewer when she was in her nineties. "I thought if I had a hobby, I could get out of here about an hour or so a week."[6]

One Sunday morning she finished getting ready for church a little early and decided to pass the time by reading the paper. And there it was, in a rare front-page advertisement: "Learn to fly."[7] Remembering her time as an airplane passenger, she quickly said to herself, "Well, that's for me. That's what I'll do. I'll learn to fly."[8]

Getting there involved almost every mode of transportation available in East Tennessee at the time. "I took a train from Jefferson City to Knoxville. The ticket cost twenty-five cents. Then I took a bus to the end of the line. That cost a dime. Then I walked about a quarter of a mile down the road, and rode in a rowboat over to Island Airport. I did that for about six months until the instructor left, then I took lessons at McGhee-Tyson [Airport]," she told Joe Godfrey, an interviewer for *AVWeb* in 1999.[9]

Her first lesson was October 1, 1944. She soloed on November 8, 1944 in a Piper J3 Cub. "No lights, no starter, no radio. I had the eight hours of dual, which was the minimum then, and the CFI (Certified Flight Instructor) got out. I'm glad nothing happened because I really didn't know a lot at that time," she said. By the following June she had earned her private pilot's license. She quickly acquired her commercial license and in 1947 became a flight instructor. On July 4, 1947, her first student soloed. Her hobby had become a business.[10]

She was barely thirty-four years old when she took that first flight. Along the way, she learned to fly seaplanes, multi-engine aircraft, and helicopters. She was the twentieth woman to become a helicopter pilot, and the fourth to become a helicopter pilot instructor. She stopped counting the number of people that she taught to fly at three thousand. She oversaw Federal Aviation Administration pilot licensing tests to well over nine thousand people. She continued flying until age ninety-seven when glaucoma and the loss of a leg in an automobile accident forced her to quit.[11]

Evelyn told Godfrey that only about five percent of the thousands of people she gave flying lessons were women. "I trained a lady that flies for American Airlines and several more that fly for freight companies and check haulers," she said. "I think the low percentage isn't because women couldn't do it, I just don't think they were that interested. If the airlines had been hiring women pilots when I came along I don't think I would have been interested in doing that. I was more interested in teaching people to fly."[12]

The source of Evelyn's nickname was a student who was not young enough to think of her as a mother substitute, Evelyn said. "One year she sent me a Mother's Day card which was funny because she's almost as old as I am," Evelyn said. "But she sent it to me because the way I looked after my students reminded her of a mama bird looking after the baby birds."[13]

Evelyn never had children of her own, although after W. J. died in 1963, she married Morgan Johnson and acquired a stepson. Morgan died in 1977.[14]

Evelyn never gave lessons to US Senator Howard H. Baker, Jr., but she did administer his pilot's license exam. And it became famous, ending up in the Congressional Record because Baker thought she was tough.[15] Here's how Evelyn relayed the story in 1999. "We were flying a Beech Debonair and when we got to the stall series he said, 'This airplane wasn't made for stalls.' I told him that if we didn't do them he'd just have to get along without his private pilot's license. He did them."[16]

Evelyn has a string of impressive honors—from being inducted into the National Aviation Hall of Fame to being named the National Flight Instructor of the Year in 1979. Two of her favorite awards include being selected for the Hamblen Women's Hall of Fame and the Carnegie Hero Award. The Hamblen Women's Hall of Fame was dear to her "because it is women that they consider to be good role models for young girls and I'm real proud of getting an award at home."[17] She was proud of receiving the Carnegie recognition because it was one of the first and it came for something she did "on impulse."[18]

The incident for which she was awarded the Carnegie Hero Award happened in 1953 when she was at the Morristown Airport. She saw a helicopter that was about fifty feet up in the air and was clearly in trouble. "I called the operator and told them to send an ambulance," she said in a StoryCorps session recorded for National Public Radio in 2010 as a former student, Adele McDonald, interviewed her.

Evelyn dragged a large fire extinguisher that was in the airport hangar close to the crashed helicopter. She got on her hands and knees and crawled under the rotor so she could turn off the engine and stop the rotor blade. A fire had started in the transmission, so she used the extinguisher to put out the fire. The owner of the helicopter was on the passenger side and clearly dead. The pilot wasn't fully conscious.

"I remembered from a first aid course that I had a few weeks before that if you move someone with a broken back that you could injure them worse or kill them. So, I didn't pull him." Instead, she concentrated on trying to bring him out of his stupor. When help got there, it took seven people to get the pilot out safely. He lived another forty-seven years, dying in old age of a heart attack.

Asked by McDonald if she was scared of the fire, Evelyn replied, "Oh, I didn't have time to be scared. I was too busy." And, of the huge fire extinguisher that she couldn't lift, "It's impulsive. You just do it. You don't stop to think, I might get killed."[19]

On her ninety-fourth birthday, during the centennial of the Wright brothers' flight at Kitty Hawk, National Public Radio's Scott Simon took a flying lesson from Evelyn. As they were in the air, Simon talked about how beautiful it was and asked if she ever got tired of it.

"No," she replied.

"Never. Never. Never."[20]

NOTES

[1] Abby Hamm, "Your Stories: Mama Bird Evelyn Johnson," WBIR, November 24, 2010, http://www.wbir.com/dontmiss/144319/207/Your-Stories-Mama-Bird-Evelyn-Johnson.

[2] tradeaplanetv, "TapTV interviews aviation legend Evelyn Bryan Johnson," February 20, 2011, http://www.youtube.com/watch?v=_GssVoBs_TQ.

[3] "Evelyn Bryan Johnson Papers 1920–2002: Archives of Appalachia." East Tennessee State University, http://www.etsu.edu/cass/archives/Collections/afindaid/a605.html.

[4] Ibid.

[5] Ibid.

[6] "Aviation World Mourns Loss of Evelyn Bryan Johnson: 'Mama Bird' was the highest-time female pilot in history," *The Spirit of Aviation,* May 14, 2012, http://www.eaa.org/news/2012/2012-05-14_johnson.asp.

[7] tradeaplanetv, "TapTV interviews aviation legend Evelyn Bryan Johnson."

[8] Ibid.

[9] Joe Godfrey, "Profile: Evelyn Bryan Johnson," *AV Web,* September 29, 1999. http://www.avweb.com/news/profiles/182968-1.html.

[10] Ibid.

[11] Dennis McLellan, "Evelyn Bryan Johnson dies at 102; pioneering female pilot: Evelyn Bryan Johnson took up flying in 1944, went on to hold a Guinness record for most hours in the air by a female pilot, and trained thousands of students," *Los Angeles Times,* May 21, 2012, http://articles.latimes.com/2012/may/21/local/la-me-evelyn-bryan-johnson-20120521.

[12] Godfrey.

[13] Ibid.

14 Staff, Obituary, *Knoxville News Sentinel,* http://www.legacy.com/obituaries/knoxnews/obituary.aspx?n=evelyn-bryan-johnson-mama-bird&pid=157555547#fb.

15 News Sentinel staff, "Aviation legend Evelyn Bryan Johnson dies at 102: East Tennessee's 'Mama Bird,'" *Knoxville News Sentinel,* May 11, 2012, http://www.knoxnews.com/news/2012/may/11/aviation-legend-evelyn-bryan-johnson-dies-102/.

16 Godfrey.

17 Ibid.

18 Brandon Hollingsworth, WUOT-FM Obituary for Evelyn Bryan Johnson includes StoryCorps Interview, May 11, 2012, transcribed by Pam Strickland. http://sunsite.utk.edu/wuot/mt/podcast/20120511JohnsonObitWEB.mp3, accessed November 15, 2012.

19 Ibid.

20 Scott Simon, "Flying with Miss Evelyn: Aloft with 'Mama Bird,' the World's Senior Flight Instructor," NPR, December 13, 2003, http://www.npr.org/templates/story/story.php?storyId=1545986.

ELMA NEAL ROANE

1918–2011

Champion of Women's Athletics

HANNAH SEAY

Courtesy of Jane R. Hooker

Elma Neal Roane

lma Neal Roane spent thirty-eight years battling for an equal
role for women's athletics at what is now the University
of Memphis. Her career as an athlete, coach, teacher, and
mentor spanned from playing in world softball championships, to
the pursuit of intercollegiate sports programs for women, to the
fight for passage of Title IX, which guaranteed the equal treatment
of women's sports at colleges across the nation.

Born August 24, 1918, in Memphis to parents Emma Neal Roane,
a nurse, and Landon Boyd Roane, an electrician, Elma was the middle child in the family.[1] Elma's family encouraged her interest in
sports, introducing her to baseball at an early age.

Elma struggled with reading in her early years, and would later
look back on that time with the realization that she was likely dys-
lexic.[2] However, the need to work harder than others in the classroom did not stop Elma and in fact may have encouraged the hard
work that led to her success.

At Messick High School in Memphis, Elma excelled in basketball
and softball, gaining All-State and All-District honors in basketball
and earning a Best Athlete award in her senior year, despite her
never growing beyond a diminutive five feet two. She also was a
member of the National Honor Society and inducted into the high
school's Best Athlete Hall of Fame.[3]

Elma was eager to continue her athletic career in college.
However, when she arrived at the West Tennessee State Teacher's
College (now the University of Memphis), Elma was devastated to
find that the school was cutting intercollegiate sports for women.[4]
Instead, Elma participated in intramural sports playing basket-
ball, softball, and tennis on teams sponsored by the college and the
Memphis Parks Commission.

During her summers, Elma continued to play amateur softball. Her prowess on the field led to her being drafted onto a

national team. She participated in the World Amateur Softball Championships for three years, 1937–1939, playing on Soldier Field in Chicago before thousands of spectators. The media frequently referred to Elma as "the best softball player in Dixie," and at the end of her softball career, she had a .500 lifetime batting average and a fielding percentage of .982.[5]

Elma fought the perception of women as the "weaker sex" all her life. In a taped interview, Elma recalled that as she entered her college years, some people had the perception that "women did not have the ability to deal with the pressure of competition, and they should not be in competition. Believe it or not, a lot of the women physical educators accepted that," Elma continued. "But I had already played at Soldier Field, and I thought that was the dumbest thing I've ever heard in my life." [6]

Elma taught physical education at the college's campus teaching school and was a star athlete, captain, and manager on the school's intramural basketball team, receiving the Best Sport Award.[7]

Elma graduated from the teacher's college with a bachelor's degree in mathematics in 1940, with additional coursework in physical education. She was on the dean's list, selected for an entry in Who's Who in American Colleges and Universities, and named Best Female Athlete.[8] After graduation, Elma taught math, girls' physical education, and coached sports at Treadwell High School in Memphis for six years, from 1940 to 1946.[9]

During those years when men left to serve overseas during World War II, Elma, along with women all over the country, filled in the gaps at home. Elma taught the junior boys' basketball team at Treadwell, and served as an assistant to the football team. The basketball team won both the city and district championships during her time as coach.[10]

Elma furthered her physical education studies during the summers at the University of Tennessee, Knoxville, with the help of a public health scholarship. She completed her master's degree in health and physical education in 1943.[11]

In 1946, Elma returned to her college campus, now named Memphis State College, where she was hired as a physical education instructor. Elma would continue her career at the university for the next thirty-eight years, taking on new responsibilities and titles until retiring as assistant athletic director and head of women's athletics in 1984.[12]

During her time at the university, Elma worked tirelessly as an educator, coach, and mentor. She coached women's basketball, volleyball, and badminton from 1955 to 1970.[13] "Physical education got a lot of flak as a 'frill' area, but to Elma it was just part of the training to be a teacher," said colleague and longtime friend Dr. Jane Hooker.[14]

In her acceptance speech as Educator of the Year at Memphis State in 1984, Elma said her experiences "have led me to believe that approximately ten percent of students are totally self-motivated and will achieve in spite of their teachers, ten percent for various reasons are rarely motivated even with the best of teaching. That leaves eighty percent that go either way. It goes without saying I was one of the eighty percent. That is the reason I think well-trained, motivated teachers are a must if we are to achieve the educational goals our city, state, and country so desperately need."[15]

"She taught us how to test and measure students, to encourage those who were not as skilled as the others," Hooker said. "She had great patience." Elma believed in the teacher-coach model, and thought that women would benefit from being physically active throughout their lives, Hooker added. Elma saw other opportunities for women in athletics as well. She trained women to be referees, and foresaw a time when women could routinely serve as game officials, sportscasters, and in team management.

Elma also took her women intramural teams on the road, organizing play dates at other college campuses in the state and hosting volleyball and badminton tournaments. Those events not only provided more training, but also served as fundraisers and public relations events, since the participants often came back as spectators for the women's college games. "We called it 'extra-murals'," Hooker quipped.

Many of these young women had never traveled beyond Memphis, but with Elma, they visited Middle and East Tennessee, learned to order in restaurants, to handle money, and to be independent, Hooker explained. Elma also used her knowledge and training in mathematics to teach her students how to budget for equipment and travel.

As Elma networked with other teachers, coaches, and administrators at campuses across the state, these women decided to form a group to support college athletics for women. Elma helped found the Tennessee College Women's Sports Federation in 1969, with the goal of reinforcing and reinstating intercollegiate athletics for women. The first year, twenty-three colleges joined. Elma served as the federation's second president.[16]

Elma was also closely involved with the national Association of Intercollegiate Athletics for Women, formed in 1971 to govern women's college athletics and to sponsor national tournaments. It was the equivalent to the National Collegiate Athletic Association, which continued at the time to exclude women's sports.[17]

In 1972, the passage of Title IX was a watershed event for women's athletics — but one that was fought tooth-and-nail by the NCAA and by many colleges themselves. This federal law requires schools to provide gender equity for any educational program that receives financial aid from the government.[18]

Elma and other proponents of the law likened Title IX to a key civil rights law for women, and without the African American civil rights struggle years earlier, it might not have stood the test of time.

"The NCAA fought it all along until they realized they weren't going to win," Elma recalled. "But when they recognized that [Title IX] wasn't going to change, then the college presidents decided that we would be in the NCAA, and that involves scholarships."[19]

During her last years at Memphis State, Elma oversaw the merger of men's and women's athletics into one department. Even after her retirement, she remained active on the boards of many athletic organizations and played sports such as golf into her eighties.[20]

"Ms. Roane deserves the credit for women's athletics at the University of Memphis," said University of Memphis President Shirley Raines. "She shaped generations of young women's lives, and countless young leaders were influenced by her depth of character, determination against great odds, and abiding belief in the power of education to change lives."[21]

In 1993, the University of Memphis renamed the athletic arena and health and sports sciences building where Elma had spent so many years as an educator and coach as the Elma Roane Fieldhouse. Today it remains the home court of the Lady Tigers.[22]

Elma passed away on September 19, 2011, at the age of ninety-three.[23] Over the years, she received numerous honors and awards for her personal and professional accomplishments.[24] However, Elma's greatest legacy is a living one — the teachers, coaches, athletes, and other successful adults who count her as a mentor and a friend. These professionals pass on Elma's life lessons each day, inspiring new generations to succeed as athletes, teachers, and role models.

NOTES

[1] Staff Reports, Obituaries, "Elma Neal Roane," *Commercial Appeal*, September 21, 2011, http://www.commercialappeal.com/news/2011/sep/21/memphis-area-obituaries-sept-21-2011.

[2] Video recording of interview with Elma Neal Roane, http://theprojectnoah.org/?p=49.

[3] Resume of Elma Neal Roane, 1972–73, Tennessee College Women's Sports Federation and Allied Organization Papers, John Willard Brister Library, University of Memphis.

[4] Marion W. Morgan, "Elma Roane was Game Changer for Women at University of Memphis," *Commercial Appeal*, September 21, 2011, http://www.commercialappeal.com/news/2011/sep21/roane-was-game-changer-for-women.

[5] Memorial service program for Elma Neal Roane, September 23, 2011.

[6] Video recording of interview with Elma Neal Roane, http://theprojectnoah.org/?p=49.

[7] Jane Hooker, "Remember When," key events of the life of Elma Neal Roane, received May 30, 2012.

[8] Jane Hooker, "Vitae, Elma Neal Roane," compiled 2011.

[9] Ibid.

[10] Adam Douglas, "Women's Athletics Pioneer Elma Roane Passes Away," *Daily Helmsman*, University of Memphis, September 20, 2011, http://www.dailyhelmsman.com/news/women-s-athletics-pioneer-elma-roane-passes-away.

[11] Staff, Obituaries, "Elma Neal Roane (1943)," University of Tennessee-Knoxville, *Torchbearer*, December 6, 2011, http://www.utk/edu/torchbearer.2011/12/elma-neal-roane-1943.

[12] Staff Reports, Obituaries, "Elma Neal Roane," *Commercial Appeal*, September 21, 2011, http://www.commercialappeal.com/news/2011/sep/21/memphis-area-obituaries-sept-21-2011.

[13] Marion W. Morgan, "Elma Roane was Game Changer for Women at University of Memphis," *Commercial Appeal*, September 21, 2011, http://www.commercialappeal.com/news/2011/sep21/roane-was-game-changer-for-women.

[14] Jane Hooker (Associate Professor Emeritus, University of Memphis), telephone interview by Hannah Seay, June 22, 2012.

[15] Transcript of speech presented by Elma Neal Roane, University of Memphis Educator of the Year awards ceremony, February 16, 1984.

[16] Staff, Obituaries, "Elma Neal Roane (1943)," University of Tennessee-Knoxville, *Torchbearer,* December 6, 2011, http://www.utk/edu/torchbearer.2011/12/elma-neal-roane-1943.

[17] History, Association of Intercollegiate Athletics for Women, Hoopedia website, http://hoopedia.nba.com/index.php?title=Association_for_Intercollegiate_Athletics_for_Women.

[18] Title IX Legislative Chronology, Women's Sports Foundation website, http://www.womenssportsfoundation.org/home/advocate/title-ix-and-issues/history-of-title-ix/history-of-title-ix.

[19] Video recording of interview with Elma Neal Roane, http://theprojectnoah.org/?p=49.

[20] Staff Reports, Obituaries, "Elma Neal Roane," *Commercial Appeal,* September 21, 2011, http://www.commercialappeal.com/news/2011/sep/21/memphis-area-obituaries-sept-21-2011.

[21] Staff, "University Mourns Passing of Elma Roane, Pioneer in Women's Athletics," *University of Memphis News,* September 21, 2011, http://www.memphis.edu/mediaroom/releases/sep11/roane.php.

[22] Adam Douglas, "Women's Athletics Pioneer Elma Roane Passes Away," *Daily Helmsman,* University of Memphis, September 20, 2011, http://www.dailyhelmsman.com/news/women-s-athletics-pioneer-elma-roane-passes-away.

[23] Obituary and memorial service program for Elma Neal Roane, September 23, 2011.

[24] Among these: University of Memphis "M" Club Hall of Fame (first female inductee); Tennessee Sports Hall of Fame; Memphis Parks Commission Hall of Fame; University of Memphis Educator of the Year; National Association of Collegiate Women Athletics Administrators' Lifetime Achievement Award; 50 Women Who Make a Difference Award by Memphis Woman magazine; Society of the Shield at the University of Memphis; 50-year Achievement Award and Outstanding Service Award by the University of Memphis National Alumni Association; and the establishment of the Elma Neal Roane Outstanding Athlete award and the Elma Neal Roane Scholarships at the University of Memphis. Source: Staff Reports, Obituaries, "Elma Neal Roane," *Commercial Appeal,* September 21, 2011, http://www.commercialappeal.com/news/2011/sep/21/memphis-area-obituaries-sept-21-2011.

CAROL LYNN GILMER YELLIN

1920–1999

Conscience of the Mid-South

JANANN SHERMAN

Yellin Family Photo

Carol Lynn Yellin

Her greatest legacy was her manifold efforts on behalf of social and racial justice, including a life of activism, a chronicle of women's rights' struggles, and a massive archival collection of the civil rights movement in Memphis. Upon her death, an editorial deemed her "a bona fide Renaissance woman" and "a resident conscience of the Mid-South."[1]

Carol Lynn Gilmer was born March 3, 1920, in Clinton, Oklahoma, a rural hamlet about eighty miles west of Oklahoma City. In an era when few women attended college, she earned a bachelor's degree in history and a master's degree in journalism from Northwestern University in 1942.

At what turned out to be a fortuitous time for young women with career aspirations, she took a job as an editor with *Reader's Digest* in New York. Carol Lynn later described herself as an "editorial Rosie the Riveter," acknowledging she could not have gotten the job at *Reader's Digest* if their male editors had not gone to war.

However, as the war unfolded, she became impatient with her life on the outside of the war looking in; so she joined the Red Cross and soon found herself on the island of Saipan serving up coffee and donuts to lonely GIs. Letters she wrote during that period later inspired her daughter, Emily, to write *Our Mother's War: American Women at Home and at the Front During World War II.*

In 1950, Carol Lynn married theater producer and broadcaster David Yellin, after an earlier failed marriage to *Mr. Roberts* author Tom Heggen. While rearing their four children—sons Tom, Chuck, Doug, and daughter, Emily—Carol Lynn continued her work as a freelance writer for *Vogue, Harper's Magazine,* and *Redbook* and as a special projects editor for *Reader's Digest Condensed Books.* Her husband, eagerly taking sides in the public controversy about women's roles in the 1950s, published an article in *Harper's* in 1956 proudly entitled "I'm Married to a Working Woman."

In 1964, the Yellins were lured to Memphis with a job offer for David to establish the film and broadcasting department at then Memphis State University. As a result, the family landed in the Mid-South in the midst of the turmoil of civil rights. They joined a cadre of white citizens determined to participate on the side of social justice. Carol Lynn was particularly active in these pursuits. One example was her engagement with the Saturday Luncheon Club, a group of black and white women who tested integration laws by meeting together for lunch at some of the finer dining establishments in the city, thereby quietly desegregating them.

Signaling her intense interest in civil rights violations wherever they occurred, Carol Lynn coauthored a book on Virginia's massive resistance to school integration called *Bound for Freedom: an educator's adventures in Prince Edward County, Virginia.* The book was nominated for a Pulitzer Prize in 1965.

The Yellins' singular achievement for civil rights began to unfold with the assassination of Dr. Martin Luther King, Jr. in Memphis on April 4, 1968. Three days later, David and Carol Lynn founded the ad hoc Memphis Search for Meaning Committee, composed of some eighty members with ties to many parts of the community, both black and white, all of them seeking to understand how and why King was killed.

As one member, Joan Turner Beifuss, noted in her definitive account of that tumultuous period, *At the River I Stand,* "Its members understood only dimly *what* had gone wrong and even less *how* and *why* the drama of labor dispute to racial crisis to catastrophe had played out all around them. But two things they were sure of. They had been witness to an important moment in American history. And it was crucial both for them and for their city to understand what happened."[2]

Members began the massive effort of documenting the city in turmoil while the feelings and materials were fresh. Ultimately, they gathered a vast multi-format collection including clippings from local news coverage and general interest magazine stories, over 150 oral history interviews with participants and observers, copies of hate mail, overheard conspiracy theories, sick jokes, radio news broadcasts, television news coverage and outtake films, still photographs, and a bloodied "I Am A Man" poster. Under a grant from the National Endowment for the Humanities, the Yellins organized the collection, formally called *The Memphis Multi-Media Archival Project: the 1968 Sanitation Workers' Strike,* now housed in the McWherter Library of the University of Memphis. Dozens of scholars researching and writing about civil rights and numerous documentary filmmakers have consulted and used these rich resources.

Acting upon their beliefs in the value of public discussion of important issues, Carol Lynn and David Yellin coproduced a WMC-TV public affairs television program called *Face to Face,* which was aired for eighteen years in the 1970s and 1980s. The Yellins were also instrumental in convincing local television to give African Americans a voice on TV, resulting in a program called *Forty Percent Speaks.*

For all their efforts on behalf of civil rights and racial justice, Carol Lynn and David Yellin were jointly awarded the Martin Luther King, Jr. Human Rights Award in 1988 from the University of Memphis.

To Carol Lynn, securing women's rights, as well as civil rights, required public action. She marched on the county courthouse to press for women on juries; she launched a long struggle with the public library to have her library card issued in the name of Carol Yellin rather than Mrs. David Yellin. And in a rare show of feminist solidarity, David Yellin went to court and legally took his wife's maiden name, Gilmer, as a gift in honor of their twenty-first wedding anniversary in 1971.

Carol Lynn eagerly attended the very First World Conference on Women, sponsored by the United Nations, June 19 to July 2, 1975, in Mexico City. This first world conference on the status of women convened some four thousand women to coincide with the 1975 International Women's Year. Two years later, in November 1977, she celebrated National Women's Year at the National Women's Conference in Houston with over twenty thousand women riding the optimistic momentum of the Equal Rights Amendment.

In between these international meetings, Carol Lynn participated in the Tennessee Women's Meeting in Clarksville, where, inspired by the women's movement admonition to uncover and tell the history of women, she helped to write and edit *Tennessee Women: Past and Present*.[3]

Carol Lynn had a particular passion for the story of woman suffrage because, as she often noted, she was born before women were granted the right to vote. In the Tennessee archives, she uncovered the astonishing and untold story of the chaotic battle in Nashville over the ratification of the Nineteenth Amendment, which ultimately passed the state, and the nation, on the strength of a single vote.

Her hour-by-hour account of those few weeks in August 1920, the frequently bitter battle and its nail-biting conclusion, was published as "Countdown in Tennessee" in *American Heritage* magazine, December 1978.[4] Though she expected this to be the genesis of a fuller study of the woman suffrage movement, she was one of eight editors chosen by *Reader's Digest* to work on a condensed Bible, so the suffrage story would have to wait.

Her local activism, however, continued unabated. She organized pro-equality luncheons and a citywide celebration on the anniversary of woman suffrage during the Equal Rights Amendment ratifying campaign, making explicit the connections between suffrage and women's equality. She also helped found the Memphis Chapter of Women in Communications, Inc., and was a co-founder and past president of the Economic Justice for Women Coalition. She led Women of Achievement, Inc., which recognizes local women for their work in bringing about change in the community. She was honored in 1989 with their Vision award "for a woman whose sensitivity to women's needs led her to tremendous achievements for women."[5]

In 1994, in anticipation of the seventy-fifth anniversary of the passage and ratification of the Nineteenth Amendment, Tennessee Governor Don Sundquist appointed a Tennessee Commemorative Woman Suffrage Commission of leading women from across the state and charged them with telling the story of Tennessee's pivotal role in the passage of this critical legislation.

Commission members from Memphis, Carol Lynn Yellin, Paula Casey, and Janann Sherman, took up the challenge and produced a museum exhibit and book, *The Perfect 36: Tennessee Delivers Woman Suffrage*, which featured Carol Lynn's hour-by-hour analysis of what happened in Tennessee and Janann Sherman's overview of women's rights struggles since the founding of the republic. Also included were analyses of arguments for and against suffrage, political cartoons, capsule biographies of suffrage activists in Tennessee, and photographs from *The Perfect 36* exhibit at the University of Memphis. Paula raised the funds to produce the book and distribute it free to every school, college, and library in the state of Tennessee.[6]

It was Carol Lynn's last project. She lived long enough to enjoy some public talks and book signings, secure in the knowledge that she had both lived history and written it. She died of cancer in March 1999 at the age of seventy-nine.

Her husband, David, died of Parkinson's disease in June 2002 at age eighty-six. They are survived by three of their four children: Tom, award-winning documentarian and executive producer for ABC News; Doug, executive producer for Iwerks Entertainment; Emily, freelance journalist and author of *Our Mothers' War* (2004) and *Your Call is (Not That) Important to Us* (2009); son Chuck, an internet pathfinder, died in 2000.

NOTES

[1] John Beifuss, *Memphis Flyer*, March 14, 1999.

[2] Joan Turner Beifuss, *At the River I Stand* (Memphis: St. Lukes Press, 1990), 461.

[3] Carol Lynn Yellin, ed., *Tennessee Women: Past and Present* (Memphis: International Women's Year Coordinating Committee and Tennessee Committee for the Humanities, 1977).

[4] Carol Lynn Yellin, "Countdown in Tennessee," *American Heritage* (December 1978).

[5] Deborah M. Clubb, ed., *A Legacy of Achievers: Women of Achievement, 1985–1994* (Memphis: Women of Achievement, Inc., 1994), 7. 105.

[6] Carol Lynn Yellin and Janann Sherman, *The Perfect 36: Tennessee Delivers Woman Suffrage* (Oak Ridge, TN: Iris Press, 1998).

ACKNOWLEDGMENTS

We are grateful to the organizations and numerous individuals who helped the Tennessee Women Project reach its goal of publishing a book on historic Tennessee women. Our dependable supporters are AAUW of Tennessee; Middle Tennessee State University, History Department; Tennessee Economic Council on Women; Tennessee Women's Political Caucus; University of Tennessee, Chattanooga, Women's Studies Program; Women's Economic Council Foundation; Women's Equity Foundation; and YWCA of Knoxville. Advisory Council members — Sara Baker, Sandra Bennett, Carole Stanford Bucy, Paula F. Casey, Janice M. Leone, Anne Loy, Rebecca Cawood McIntyre, Marcia Noe, Patricia Pierce, Alma Sanford, Hannah Seay, and Yvonne Wood — assisted us throughout the project, and we benefitted greatly from their experience, expertise, and insights.

We thank the twenty contributors who generously agreed to fit this project into their already busy schedules. They infused the profiles with enthusiasm and energy.

Readers who provided helpful comments and suggestions on early drafts include: Marietta Anderson, Rose-Linda Baldwin, Sidna Bookout, Cassandra Bennett, Mona Brittingham, Pat Clark, Karen Coleman, Alex Collins, Clare Crawford, Lara Crawford,

Mayme Crowell, Kathy Desjarlais, Autumn Hall, Ann Indingaro, Patricia Knight, Elizabeth Lambert, Nancy Lantz, Connie Malarkey, Gail Mattson, Marcia Noe, Mandi Pitt-Read, Angela Quick, Jessica Reeves, Linda Richards, Stephanie Seay, Cynthia Serbin, Rachel Shope, Angela Sirna, and Gretta Stanger.

We appreciate help from descendants and family members of the women profiled: Geoff Duggan, Fred Heddleson, John M. Jones, Jr., Bruce Ross, Bette Wheeler-Strictland, and Emily Yellin.

These colleagues and friends of the women profiled charitably shared information, personal stories, documents, and perspectives: Roger Cloutier, retired director, Professional Training Division, Oak Ridge Associated Universities; Genevieve Roessler, professor emeritus, Nuclear Engineering Department, Florida State University; John Noakes, director, Center for Applied Isotope Studies, University of Georgia; Jane Hooker, associate professor emeritus, Memphis State University; and Paula Casey, editorial coordinator of *The Perfect 36: Tennessee Delivers Woman Suffrage*.

Lauren Schaubhut, curator of collections, Sam Houston Memorial Museum; Bill Stevens, librarian, Lincoln Memorial University; Shirley Hall, Baker's Creek Presbyterian Church; and Joyce McDaniel, partner in The Ferrell McDaniel Company, provided special research assistance.

We received financial support from AAUW of Tennessee and the Tennessee Women's Political Caucus as well as donations from many individuals. The Women's Equity Foundation, an organization whose mission is to promote education and equity for women and girls in Tennessee, awarded a grant to the Tennessee Women Project.

We express our sincere thanks for the support, encouragement, and assistance we have received. This has been a personally rewarding experience and we have learned and enjoyed new aspects of Tennessee history.

SELECTED BIBLIOGRAPHY

W e list here some of the writings used in *Tennessee Women of Vision and Courage*. This bibliography is by no means a complete record of all the works and sources consulted. It intends to serve as a convenience for those seeking readily available information about our historic Tennessee women. A separate list of online sources follows the selected bibliography. Those looking for specialized resources are encouraged to consult the extensive endnotes supplied by contributors.

"Anna Belle Clement O'Brien Calls Upon Democrats to Work Harder for Candidates." *Greeneville Sun* (April 1, 2009).

Beach, Ursula Smith. *Along the Warioto or a History of Montgomery County, Tennessee.* Nashville: McQuiddy Press, 1964.

Brewer, Alberta and Carson Brewer. *Valley So Wild, A Folk History.* Knoxville: East Tennessee Historical Society, 1975.

Bucy, Carole. *A History of Metro Government: Then & Now.* Brentwood: Moss Rose Press, 2013.

"Clarksville's Newest Bank Opens." *Leaf Chronicle* (Oct. 6, 1919) Clarksville, TN: Austin Peay State University Felix G. Woodward Library Microfilm.

Gaston, Kay Baker. *Emma Bell Miles.* Signal Mountain, TN: Walden's Ridge Historical Association, 1985.

Hine, Darlene Clark, Rosalyn Terborg-Penn, and Elsa Barkley Brown, eds. "Julia Britton Hooks." In *Black Women in America: An Historical Encyclopedia*. Bloomington: Indiana University Press, 1993.

Houston, General Sam. *Life of General Sam Houston, A Short Autobiography*. Austin, Texas: The Pemberton Press, 1964.

Howes, Ruth H. and Caroline L. Herzenberg. *Their Day in the Sun, Women of The Manhattan Project*. Philadelphia: Temple University, 2003.

Hubbard, Rita Lorraine. *African Americans of Chattanooga: A History of Unsung Heroes*. Charleston, SC: The History Press, 2008. 93–96.

"John Burnett's Account." *The Chronicles of Oklahoma*. 2002: 337-341.

Jones, John M. and Gregg K. Jones. "Memorials." *Historic Greene County, Tennessee and Its People: 1783–1992*. 1992: 414.

Lane, Margaret. *Frances Wright and the Great Experiment*. Totowa, NJ: Rowman & Littlefield, 1972.

Levine, Susan. *Degrees of Equality*. Philadelphia: Temple University Press, 1995.

Lewis, Selma and Marjean G. Kremer. *The Angel of Beale Street: A Biography of Julia Ann Hooks*. St. Luke's Press, 1986.

McIntyre, Rebecca Cawood and Nancy Rupprecht. "Learn to Stand Alone: Women on Campus." In *Middle Tennessee State University, A Centennial Legacy*, edited by Janice Leone. Nashville: Twin Oaks Press, 2011. 53–86.

Miles, Emma Bell. *The Spirit of the Mountains*. Knoxville: The University of Tennessee Press, 1975.

Montgomery, James Riley, Stanley J. Folmsbee, and Lee Seifert Green. *To Foster Knowledge: A History of the University of Tennessee, 1794–1970*. Knoxville: University of Tennessee.

Morris, Celia. *Fanny Wright: Rebel in America*. Cambridge: Harvard University Press, 1984.

Perdue, Theda and Michael D. Green. *The Cherokee Nation and The Trail of Tears*. New York: Viking, 2007.

Pitts, John. "Washington Probes MTSU Job Bias." *Sidelines* 50, no. 3 (June 22, 1976): 1.

Roane, Elma Neal. Resume, 1972–73. Tennessee College Women's Sports Federation and Allied Organization Papers. John Willard Brister Library. University of Memphis.

Rona, Elizabeth. *How It Came About: Radioactivity, Nuclear Physics, Atomic Energy.* Oak Ridge, Tennessee: Oak Ridge Associated Universities, 1978.

Sawyer, Susan. *More than Petticoats: Remarkable Tennessee Women.* Helena, Montana: Falcon Publishing, 2000.

Smith, D. Ray. "Peggy Heddleson—A True Artist with a Passion for Banners." Historically Speaking. *The Oak Ridger* (March 31, 2011).

Smith, Jessie Carney, editor. *Notable Black American Women, Book II.* Thomson Gale, 1996.

Susong, Edith O'Keefe. "But, 'The Democrat' Survived." *The Greeneville Sun Centennial Edition* (July 1979): 56.

Taylor, A. Elizabeth. *The Woman Suffrage Movement in Tennessee.* New York: Bookman Associates, 1957.

"The Susan B. Riley Scholarship." *Peabody Reflector* (Fall 2009).

Van West, Carroll, ed. *Tennessee Encyclopedia of History & Culture.* Nashville: Rutledge Hill Press, 1998.

"Writers and Literary Clubs." In *Heart of the Valley: A History of Knoxville, Tennessee,* edited by Lucille Deaderick. Knoxville: East Tennessee Historical Society, 1976, 452-453.

Yellin, Carol Lynn and Janann Sherman. *The Perfect 36: Tennessee Delivers Woman Suffrage.* Oak Ridge, TN: Iris Press, 1998.

Yellin, Carol Lynn. "Countdown in Tennessee." *American Heritage* (December 1978).

Yellin, Emily. *Our Mothers' War: American Women at Home and at the Front During World War II.* New York: Free Press, 2004.

ONLINE SOURCES

With the advent of the internet, many valuable resources are available online. This list of online sources is by no means a complete record of all that were accessed by our contributors. Readers may find it difficult to retrieve some of these sources as website addresses change and material is sometimes deleted or altered. However, there is a vast amount of excellent material available online for the discerning researcher.

AAUW online Museum. https://svc.aauw.org/museum/history/1950_1959/ index.cfm.

"Archive Record." January 2011. http://cherokeemuseum.pastperfect-online.com/356cgi/mweb.exe?request=record;id=241#5834-7C92-41F9-A7BB1322523914381;type=3011.

Burstein, Patricia. "Never Fear—Livia's Here! and the New Women's Bank Is Opening Its Doors." *People* Archive 4, no. 16 (Oct. 20, 1975). www.People.com/people/archive/article.

"Declaration of Sentiments and Resolutions of the Woman's Rights Convention, Held at Seneca Falls, 19–20 July 1848." *The Selected Papers of Elizabeth Cady Stanton & Susan B. Anthony.* Vol. 1. New Brunswick, NJ: Rutgers UP, 1997. The Elizabeth Cady Stanton & Susan B. Anthony Papers Project. http://ecssba.rutgers.edu/docs/seneca.html/.

"Evelyn Bryan Johnson Papers 1920–2002: Archives of Appalachia." East Tennessee State University. http://www.etsu.edu/cass/archives/Collections/afindaid/a605.html.

Haley, James T. *Afro-American Encyclopaedia: Or, the Thoughts, Doings, and Sayings of the Race.* Nashville: Haley & Florida, 1895, 332-564. Online through University of North Carolina, "Documenting the American South." http://docsouth.unc.edu/church/haley/haley.html

Ham, Abby. "Your Stories: Mama Bird Evelyn Bryan Johnson." WBIR. http://www.wbir.com/dontmiss/144319/207/Your-Stories-Mama-Bird-Evelyn-Johnson.

"History of the Association of Intercollegiate Athletics for Women." Hoopedia website. http://hoopedia.nba.com/index.php?title=Association_for_Intercollegiate_Athletics_for_Women.

Hollingsworth, Brandon. WUOT-FM Obituary for Evelyn Bryan Johnson includes StoryCorps Interview. May 11, 2012. http://sunsite.utk.edu/wuot/mt/podcast/20120511JohnsonObitWEB.mp3.

"How 'Mama Bird' Gave Me Wings: A Tribute to Evelyn Bryan Johnson." *Breaking through the Clouds.* May 11, 2012. http://breakingthrough-clouds.wordpress.com/tag/evelyn-bryan-johnson/.

Monticello Research & Collections. "Francis Wright" in *Thomas Jefferson Encyclopedia.* http://www.monticello.org/site/research-and-collections/frances-wright.

Riley, Susan B. "Knowing the South through Books." *Peabody Journal of Education,* 18, 1, 1940. http://www.tandfonline.com/doi/abs/10.1080/01619564009535607.

Roane, Elma Neal. Video recording of interview, Neighborhood Older Adult History project. Sponsored by the Highland Area Renewal Corporation. Last modified August 21, 2008, http://theprojectnoah.org/?p=49.

Simon, Scott. "Flying with Miss Johnson Aloft with 'Mama Bird,' the World's Senior Flight Instructor." NPR. December 13, 2003. http://www.npr.org/templates/story/story.php?storyId=1545986

Tennessee History Classroom, A woman's right to vote, The story of Lizzie Crozier French. http://www.tennesseehistory.com/class/LizzieCrozier.htm.

The Tennessee Encyclopedia of History and Culture. Version 2.0. http://tennesseeencyclopedia.net/entry.php?rec=1528/.

Title IX Legislative Chronology. Women's Sports Foundation. http://www.womenssportsfoundation.org/home/advocate/title-ix-and-issues/history-of-title-ix/history-of-title-ix.

"Treasures of American History: Woman Suffrage." Smithsonian National Museum of American History. http://americanhistory.si.edu/exhibitions/small_exhibition.cfm?key=1267&exkey=143&pagekey=242/.

Contributors

Twenty women from Tennessee, all with writing experience and from a variety of professional backgrounds, volunteered to research, document, and create original profiles of the twenty-two historic Tennessee women included in this book. Each contributor drew from her own unique knowledge and experience to connect with her subject and make history come alive.

Four contributors knew their subject personally. Carole Bucy was acquainted with Molly Todd as a social activist in Nashville. Ann Thornfield-Long admired Peggy Heddleson's beautiful banners with their meaningful phrases. Margaret Jane Powers knew Anna Belle Clement O'Brien as a friend, supporter, and mentor. Janann Sherman worked closely with Carol Lynn Yellin in writing *The Perfect 36: Tennessee Delivers Woman Suffrage.*

Four contributors interviewed descendants of the women they profiled. Judy Arnold interviewed Bruce Ross who helped her separate legend from fact about his great-great-grandmother, Quatie Ross. Margie LeCoultre met with John M. Jones, Jr., executive editor of *The Greeneville Sun,* the newspaper his grandmother, Edith O'Keefe Susong, rescued and made into the success that continues today. Rita Hubbard talked with the daughter of Emma Rochelle Wheeler who was very helpful. Kathy Duggan, whose husband Geoff is a descendant of Angie Warren Perkins, had access to family papers and documents about Perkins.

Other writers conducted interviews with persons who had known the subject personally. Patricia Hope interviewed past colleagues of Elizabeth Rona's. Rebecca McIntyre, a faculty member at Middle Tennessee State University, had first-hand knowledge of June Anderson's impact there, and she talked with faculty members who had known Anderson. Hannah Seay learned much about Elma Neal Roane through contacts with Jane Hooker who had been a friend and colleague of Roane's.

Several contributors connected with their subjects through place. Deborah Staley lives near the historic site in Blount County where Elizabeth Houston raised her family. Stephanie Todd lives in Chattanooga near the mountains that inspired Emma Bell Miles. Sara Baker discovered that Fanny Wright's grave is in a cemetery located in her hometown of Cincinnati. Taylor Emery lives in Clarksville where Brenda Runyon established the first bank in the nation run by women.

Ayne Cantrell used her one-act play depicting a suffragist rally to capture the essence of the suffragist movement in Tennessee. Paula Casey drew from her extensive knowledge about the suffragist movement in Tennessee history to write the introduction to the play and profiles about the play's four suffragist characters—Lide Smith Meriwether, Martha Moore Allen, Anne Dallas Dudley, and Sue Shelton White.

Sherri Gardner Howell and Pam Strickland brought their journalistic skills to the stories of Julia Britton Hooks and Evelyn Bryan Johnson. Strickland gives us an example of research capabilities that are now readily available—all her citations came from online sources. Margaret Emmett, a long-time AAUW member and leader, contributed her unique insights and knowledge in writing about Susan B. Riley, an inspiring faculty member at Peabody College (now part of Vanderbilt University) and the only Tennessee woman to become national president of AAUW.

These twenty contemporary writers have created a living history. In many instances, they recorded oral history that might have been lost were it not for their efforts. Their narratives about these resolute twenty-two historic women make a valuable contribution to not only Tennessee women's history but to the appreciation of the fortitude of our Tennessee foremothers.

Judy Arnold began her career in 1970 as a substitute teacher. She became an English teacher/tennis coach at Knoxville's Bearden High School, coordinator of secondary field experience at the University of Tennessee, English professor and coordinator of the Oak Ridge Writing Center at Roane State Community College, and chair of the education department/women's varsity tennis coach at Tennessee Wesleyan College. She is a professor of graduate teacher education at Lincoln Memorial University and served as director of the MEd in initial licensure program. She is past president of AAUW Knoxville Branch and current chair of the equity issues task force. She has made international presentations concerning educational issues. She received Lincoln Memorial University's Houston Award for Excellence in Teaching and the YWCA Tribute to Women Award for Education. She is married to Toby Rogers, a career educator. Their daughter, Sarah, is a third generation AAUW member.

Sara Baker is a writer, editor, and consultant specializing in gender justice. She has worked for UN Women and the YWCA, taught English composition at the University of Tennessee, and taught English as a second language in Wroclaw, Poland. A believer in social justice, Sara has studied women and religion in India, started women's groups in rural Appalachia, advocated for women's health in the UK, developed empowerment programs for girls in inner-city

Philadelphia, and written news summaries on women's rights in Central Asia. She holds an MA in English from the University of Tennessee and a BA in English and religion from Maryville College.

Carole Bucy is a professor of history at Volunteer State Community College and the Davidson County Historian. She holds a PhD in American history from Vanderbilt University as well as degrees from Baylor University and George Peabody College. She is the author of several scholarly articles about Tennessee women and two textbooks for fourth and fifth grades currently on the Tennessee state adoption list. She regularly conducts teacher workshops on women's contributions to our state's history.

B. Ayne Cantrell, DA, (professor emerita, Middle Tennessee State University) retired from MTSU in 2005 where she taught English and women's studies courses for over thirty years. At MTSU Ayne received the King-Hampton Award (1991) for outstanding contributions to the advancement of women at the university and was the first recipient of the Ayne Cantrell Award (1992), an award named in her honor and given annually to outstanding women's studies faculty. For a number of years she served as president, director, and actor for the Murfreesboro Ensemble Theatre. Presently she oversees university relations for AAUW of Tennessee and serves as communications officer for the AAUW Murfreesboro Branch. A native of Lebanon, Tennessee, Ayne lives with her dog Zoe in Murfreesboro.

Paula F. Casey, a graduate of the University of Tennessee, Knoxville with a BS in communications and a rabid Lady Vols basketball fan, is a former newspaper journalist who was editorial coordinator for *The Perfect 36: Tennessee Delivers Woman Suffrage*. She produced a video/DVD on woman suffrage for the political reference files of the Smithsonian Institution, and is a dynamic speaker on voting rights. She has spoken around the country on the seventy-two-year struggle for American women to win the right to vote, the greatest nonviolent revolution in the history of our country. A thirty-six-year member of the National Federation of Press Women, she helped edit the collaborative online exhibit of the National Women's History Museum, "Women with a Deadline: Female Printers, Publishers and Journalists from the Colonial Period to World War I," honoring women's contributions to the printed word at www.nwhm.org. More information is available at www.theperfect36.com and www. paulacasey.com.

Kathy Owens Duggan is a thirty-two year award-winning veteran of the public school system. She has been a teacher, curriculum coach, and principal; and is currently the principal of Adrian Burnett Elementary School in Knoxville. A recipient of the Presidential Award for Excellence in Math and Science Teaching, Knox County Teacher of the Year, and Halls Woman of the Year Award, her passion is to inspire a desire for reading and lifelong learning in children and adults. In addition to reading and learning, Kathy enjoys traveling, golf, and gardening. She lives in Knoxville with her husband, Geoff.

Taylor Emery, a Clarksville, Tennessee, native, is a tenured instructor in the department of languages and literature at Austin Peay State University, where she teaches composition, world literature, and introduction to university classes. She has published articles in Tennessee Philological Association's *Bulletin*, *The Encyclopedia of World War I*, *The Encyclopedia of World War II*, *Kentucky Philological Review*, and a chapter in *Arthurian Writers: A*

Biographical Encyclopedia, along with numerous book reviews for *Choice Magazine.* She enjoys gardening and lives in a mid-century ranch, with her husband and rescued pets. Currently, she is attempting to learn to play the ukulele.

Margaret B. Emmett is retired from Oak Ridge National Laboratory (ORNL) where she spent fifty years working in the nuclear engineering field. Her expertise is in Monte Carlo Radiation Transport. She was group leader of nuclear code development for fifteen years, and served for over twenty years as the work force diversity representative for her ORNL division. She has long been active in AAUW, having served as branch and state president and as SouthEast Central regional director. Her state project while AAUW of Tennessee president was SHADES (SHaring ADventures in Engineering and Science) which has been very successful and has continued for twenty-one years. SHADES is a highly interactive, demonstration-oriented workshop designed to show middle-school girls that math, science, and engineering are "fun" and interesting, and career options are diverse.

Award-winning writer **Patricia A. Hope** has published widely in anthologies, magazines, newspapers, and literary journals including the online literary journal *Maypop* and a short story in *Muscadine Lines.* Her articles have appeared in *The Writer, Blue Ridge Country, An Encyclopedia of East Tennessee, These Are Our Voices, An Appalachian Studies Teacher's Manual,* and numerous more. She has written extensively for area newspapers including the *Knoxville News Sentinel* and *The Oak Ridger,* her hometown newspaper. She is past chair of the Tennessee Writers Alliance (TWA) and editor of the first TWA anthology, *A Tennessee Landscape, People, and Places.* She is past president of the East Tennessee Chapter of Society of

Professional Journalists, winner of the American Cancer Society's statewide Best Media Coverage Award and winner of a Tennessee Press Association Award. She co-founded and served as executive director of Tennessee Mountain Writers, Inc., a nonprofit writing organization.

Sherri Gardner Howell has been in journalism since she graduated from the University of Tennessee in 1976. Gardner Howell's career includes feature writer, columnist, section editor, and assistant managing editor for a major daily newspaper and publisher of a small town weekly newspaper. Gardner Howell jumped into the world of small business and sole proprietorship with the founding of SGH Enterprises in 2012. Her company offers writing services, public relations, and marketing, concentrating primarily on small businesses that need an extra push to improve their visibility and image. In her *Knoxville News Sentinel* column, Rhymes and Reasons, she writes about family and friends and navigating today's world as a woman. It has been a staple in the *News Sentinel* for twenty-five years.

Rita Lorraine Hubbard is a former educator and a long-time lover of African American history. A native Chattanoogan, Rita has been writing since she could hold a pencil. She is the author of *African Americans of Chattanooga: A History of Unsung Heroes* (The History Press, 2008), and has recently been named Lee and Low Publishers' 2012 New Voices Award winner. She worked as a researcher for NBC's "Who Do You Think You Are" featuring the life of Lionel Richie and enjoys writing middle grade and young adult historical fiction. She also manages several websites, including a personal blog called "Rita Writes History" www.RitaHubbard.com, and a children's book review blog called Picture Book Depot.

Margie Humphrey LeCoultre, EdD, began teaching in Kingsport in 1959. She moved to the Knoxville City School System in 1971 and was appointed principal in 1979. Margie continued as principal when the Knoxville city and Knox County schools merged in 1987. She retired in 2000. The Knoxville Chamber of Commerce bestowed their prestigious Best Award to the principal and faculty of three schools where Margie was principal. She and the college dean of the University of Tennessee planned the individualized instruction intern program, which she presented as guest lecturer at Northwest Wales Institute, Wrexham, Wales. Margie edited the *Knoxville Bicentennial Educators' Resource Manual: A History of Knoxville, Tennessee.* She served as local and state president of AAUW. Honors include the 1994 Carson Newman College Outstanding Alumni Community Service Award and induction into the 2013 Knoxville East High School Hall of Fame. She resides in Powell with her husband, David.

Rebecca Cawood McIntyre is an associate professor of history at Middle Tennessee State University where she teaches US history and the history of tourism. She earned her doctoral degree from The University of Alabama in 2004. In 2011, University Press of Florida published *Souvenirs of the Old South: Northern Tourism and Southern Mythology,* her book that examined the ways tourism shaped southern identity for northern visitors. That year she also authored a chapter on women at MTSU for a collection honoring the school's centennial. Currently, she serves on the advisory council of the Tennessee Women Project and works with several scholars on a Tennessee history textbook. She is past president of the Kentucky and Tennessee American Studies Association and is regional director of National History Day in Middle Tennessee. She resides in Murfreesboro with her husband and three daughters.

Margaret Jane Powers is an attorney at The Powers Law Firm, the firm she founded in 1980 in Crossville, Tennessee. She is a descendant of Colonel John Donelson, co-founder of Nashville and father of Rachel Donelson Jackson, wife of President Andrew Jackson. Powers served a two-year term as Speaker of the House of Delegates for the Tennessee Bar Association, was a founder and subsequent president of the Tennessee Lawyers Association for Women, and was selected by the dean of the University of Tennessee College of Law to serve on the Dean's Advisory Council. Powers' civic service includes helping found the Art Circle Public Library Foundation and serving three terms on the Tennessee Economic Council on Women where she was elected chair. She presently serves on the board of the Women's Fund for the Community Foundation of Middle Tennessee. She is an avid student of and participant in Tennessee's political history.

Hannah Seay is a member of the class of 2014 at the Webb School of Knoxville. In addition to honors-level coursework, Hannah works as a reporter and editor for the school newspaper *Spartan Spirit*, serves as a junior ambassador for the admissions office, is captain of the girls' varsity soccer team, and is a three-time delegate to Model United Nations. During the summers, she works as a junior counselor at Webb Day Camp. Hannah is a teacher in the religious education program and an active youth group member at Tennessee Valley Unitarian Universalist Church. She has worked as a volunteer for service projects and events of AAUW Knoxville Branch, Pond Gap Elementary Community Schools program, English for Speakers of Other Languages program, Boys and Girls Club, Volunteer Ministries, Sertoma Club, Humane Society of the Tennessee Valley, and the Knoxville Zoo.

Janann Sherman, professor emeritus of history, was the first female chair of the history department at the University of Memphis (2004–2013). She holds a PhD from Rutgers University in New Jersey, and began teaching at the University of Memphis in 1994. Sherman is author or coauthor of eight books: *The Perfect 36: Tennessee Delivers Woman Suffrage, No Place for a Woman: A Life of Senator Margaret Chase Smith, Interviews with Betty Friedan, Memphis in Black and White, Images of Beale Street, Dreamers. Thinkers. Doers: A Centennial History of the University of Memphis, The University of Memphis: A Campus History,* and *Walking on Air: The Aerial Adventures of Phoebe Omlie.*

Deborah Grace Staley, a lifelong East Tennessean, is an award-winning and best-selling fiction writer. Her latest novel, *Unforgettable,* was released by Bell Bridge Books in the fall of 2012. She holds a BA from King College and an MFA in writing from Goddard College. Married to her college sweetheart, they have one son and split their time between their home on five acres in Maryville, Tennessee, in a circa 1867 farmhouse and a condo on the Indian River in Cocoa, Florida. Deborah writes full time and teaches creative writing at Full Sail University in Winter Park, Florida.

A native of Harriman, Tennessee, **Pam Strickland** is a popular weekly op-ed columnist for the *Knoxville News Sentinel.* She has worked as a journalist covering politics and social justice issues in Tennessee and Arkansas and earned the description of a "reporter I really respected" from President Bill Clinton in his autobiography, *My Life.* Previously she contributed political commentary to KUAR-FM, 89.1, an NPR affiliate in Little Rock. Her essays are included in the anthologies *A Rough Sort of Beauty: Reflections on the Natural Heritage of Arkansas, Outscape: Writings on Fences and Frontiers,* and

Low Explosions: Writings on the Body. She is co-author of the children's book *Under One Flag: A Year at Rohwer* (August House). She has a bachelor's degree from the University of Tennessee, Knoxville and studied rhetoric and law at University of Arkansas at Little Rock. She lives in Knoxville and is active in St. James Episcopal Church.

Ann Thornfield-Long is a writer and journalist living near Knoxville, Tennessee. She holds a BA in psychology from Ball State University where she also studied journalism. She was editor/ publisher of one of the smallest weekly newspapers in the US, reported for numerous newspapers, and contributed articles to anthologies and religious publications. She worked as a licensed practical nurse and spent ten years as a medical first responder before her retirement. She enjoys spending time with her family, hiking, and traveling.

Stephanie Todd is a lecturer at the University of Tennessee at Chattanooga, teaching literature and rhetoric classes. Her scholarly interests lie in nineteenth century American literature, focusing on women nature writers.

Index

ABOUT THE EDITORS

C harlotte Crawford is an award-winning advocate for promoting educational opportunities for women and girls and furthering the professional advancement of women. In an eclectic educational career, she has taught mathematics for teens and violin lessons for pre-school children, developed standardized science achievement tests, and led workshops for parents and teachers. She spent nine years as an elected school board member, six as the first female board president. As president of one of two nonprofit foundations she cofounded, she directed statewide programs for girls, coordinated a statewide speaker's bureau, and coauthored journal articles, newsletters, and the sexual harassment prevention curricula, *Expect Respect*. She has coauthored/coedited six books on women or girls including *Fairness: A Guide to Gender Equity in Illinois Schools* as well as the historical books *Folk Crosses* and *A Year in the West: A Kansas Family's Expedition*. She lives in Farragut, Tennessee, with her husband.

Ruth Johnson Smiley, PhD, conducted her doctoral research at Oak Ridge National Laboratory and later headed a research project at Oak Ridge Associated Universities. She has written technical reports and published papers in professional journals. In addition, Ruth taught economics at Pellissippi State Community College. She served as state president of AAUW and coeditor of the *AAUW*

Tennessean. Honors include an E Award (for Excellence, Equity, and Equality) from the Tennessee Economic Council on Women in 2011, finalist in Knoxville YWCA's Tribute to Women in 2012, and recognition as a civil rights advocate by the Tennessee Human Rights Commission in 2013. A native Tennessean, she has a personal interest in Tennessee history. She researched and documented her family lineage for *First Families of Tennessee*, a project of the East Tennessee Historical Society. She and her husband, Doug Smiley, live in Oak Ridge. They enjoy gardening, hiking, kayaking, and photography.

You may contact the editors or contributors at tnwomenproject@gmail.com.

Proceeds from *Tennessee Women of Vision and Courage* provide copies of the book for public high school libraries in Tennessee and scholarships to attend the annual National Conference for College Women Student Leaders.

Made in the USA
Lexington, KY
27 February 2018